THE RAINMAKER

The Life Story of Venerable Ngagpa

Yeshe Dorje Rinpoche

THE RAINMAKER

The Life Story of Venerable Ngagpa

Yeshe Dorje Rinpoche

DR. MARSHA WOOLF
and
PROFESSOR KAREN BLANC

Foreword by
His Holiness the Dalai Lama

Afterword by
Professor Robert A.F. Thurman

SIGO PRESS
·
BOSTON

Copyright © 1994 Marsha Woolf
Karen Blanc
Venerable Yeshe Dorje Rinpoche

All rights reserved. No part of this book may be reproduced or transmitted in any form or by any means, electronic or mechanical, including photo copying, recording or by any information storage and retreival system, without permission in writing from the publisher.

3/01

SIGO PRESS
25 New Chardon Street, #8748
Boston, Massachusetts 02114

Library of Congress Card Catalog Number: 90-8809
ISBN 0-939434-28-7
ISBN 0-938434-15-2 (pbk.)
Printed in Korea

ACKNOWLEDGEMENTS

We would like to thank His Holiness the Dalai Lama; His Holiness the late Venerable Dudjom Rinpoche (the late Venerable Yeshe Dorje Rinpoche's Root Lama); Professor Robert A.F. Thurman; Kalon Tenzin Geyche Tethong; Mr. Karma Gyatsho for his major contribution as translator; Mr. Lobsang Norbu for his tireless translating at the initial interviews; Ms. Christine Klemmer Thondup, devoted student since 1978 and personal secretary of Rinpoche's since 1984, who helped in both in India and abroad; Mr. Tsering Thondup for his assistance to Rinpoche; Yeshe Dorje Rinpoche's family, especially his son Karma Sonam, who helped oversee the construction and management of the monastery, his son Karma Norbu, for his contribution to the artwork of the monastery and the drawings for this book, and his wife Mrs. Grace Wu Dorje for her support and devotion to Rinpoche; all the monks, nuns, yogis, yognis, sangha, and staff of Zilnon Kagyeling Monastery; statue maker Mr. Kelsang Dorje; and all the local Indian workers who helped to construct the monastery.

CREDITS

Historic photos of Tibet contributed by The Library of Tibetan Works and Archives, Dharamsala, India
Cover photo by Jennifer Eyre
Other photos by Philip Hemley, Marsha Woolf David Johnston, Zilnon Kagyeling Monastery
All drawings by Karma Norbu
Book design by Dr. Marsha Woolf
A special thanks to Donaia De Marco for her help with the book

All profits from this book will be sent to the Nyingmapa monastery. Now more than ever, contributions are needed. They may be sent directly to:

Zilnon Kagyeling Monastery
Above Bhagsu Road
McLeod Ganj,
Upper Dharamsala–176215
District Kangra, H.P. India

Zilnon Kagyeling Monastery
Photo courtesy of Zilnon Kagyeling Monastery

DEDICATION

We lovingly dedicate this book to the memory of Venerable Yeshe Dorje Rinpoche. He touched many hearts and many lives.

A dedicated spiritual man, he profoundly influenced many students, as well as those who attended his classes in ancient Buddhist teachings in the West.

Although he was a revered and famous weather controller, he was a humble man. Just by being in his presence, his joyful spirit and humor, love, compassion, and good will, uplifted all who knew him.

May this book serve as an example and a reminder to us all, that commitment and unfaltering dedication can lead us all to the realization of our goals.

CONTENTS

DEDICATION   vii

FOREWORD–
by His Holiness the Dalai Lama   xi

PREFACE I   xiii

PREFACE II   xvii

PROLOGUE   xxi

Chapter One–
THE EARLY YEARS   1

Chapter Two–
IN THE MONASTERY   11

Chapter Three–
MEDITATION AND RETREAT   18

Chapter Four–
JOURNEY AND RAINMAKING   25

Chapter Five–
TRANSMUTATION, THE CHINESE
INVASION, AND EXILE FROM TIBET   35

Chapter Six–
LIFE IN INDIA   49

Chapter Seven— BUILDING THE MONASTERY	62
EPILOGUE	73
INTERVIEW— On Meditation with Venerable Yeshe Dorje Rinpoche by Dr. Marsha Woolf	75
APPENDIX— Commentary on Tibetan Buddhism by His Holiness the Dalai Lama	83
AFTERWORD— Tibet Today by Professor Robert A.F. Thurman	91
GLOSSARY	96
BIBLIOGRAPHY	99
MAP OF INDIAN UNION	101
ABOUT THE AUTHORS	102

THE DALAI LAMA

FOREWORD

Tibetan Buddhism is rich in spiritual traditions, including a wide variety of ways to lead a religious life. This comes about not only because individuals differ in their inclinations and abilities, but also because of the different needs of society. Although the monastic community has always been of fundamental importance, ever since Buddhism was first introduced to Tibet from India there has also been a role for dedicated practitioners. This book contains the story of one such man, who followed the path of an itinerant meditator. Wandering from place to place, he would meditate in caves and remote places, dependent on the support of the local people. They in turn would request him to perform rituals for their welfare. His particular skill, the prevention and summoning of rain, had special value in Tibet, where drought on the one hand and violent hailstorms on the other could have a drastic effect on people's lives.

Here, in India, Ngakpa Yeshe Dorje has established the Zilnon Kagyeling Monastery to preserve the spiritual lineages he represents. These include practices and teachings of the Nyingma tradition, taught by Guru Padmasambhava, the great Indian master who established Buddhism in Tibet, as well as those derived from the practices of the great Fifth Dalai Lama, who unified the Tibetan nation. At the present crucial juncture in Tibetan history, when both the Tibetan people and their religion are under threat, it is important that these traditions be maintained.

For this reason I hope that Ngakpa Yeshe Dorje's efforts will be rewarded with success.

July 30, 1992

PREFACE - Part I

I first met Venerable Yeshe Dorje Rinpoche in India in 1983 during the beginning of my fourteen-month journey throughout India and the Far East. The first stop was at Dharamsala—a hill station in Northern India—to visit, study, and work with my teacher in Tibetan medicine. One day, when Rinpoche's name came up in conversation, my teacher, Dr. Yeshi Dhonden, said that he had heard that Rinpoche had had a bad fall. When I asked if I could help, he suggested that I might offer acupuncture. Since natural medicine and acupuncture have been two of my specialties since the early 1970's, it seemed appropriate.

A Swiss man happened to be going to see Yeshe Dorje and offered to guide me up the winding mountain to his house. As I removed my shoes and entered his place, which appeared meager and humble, I saw many people sitting in front of Rinpoche asking spiritual advice. He had a kind and gentle face with a childlike twinkle in his eyes. Smiling and laughing often, he answered their questions. He had a sense of greatness about him.

My view was blocked by a pole, and as I stood in the shadows, every now and then Rinpoche would lean from side to side to peer around the pole at me. Soon we were playing a silent game like two small children, smiling at each other as he continued to answer questions. This never interfered with the seriousness of his concentration as he contemplated each question.

Dr. Dhonden had told me that Rinpoche was a famous rainmaker and weather controller, and since it has always rained or snowed on my birthday since I can remember, and many significant events and spiritual confirmations throughout my life have been marked by signs from the elements, I was fascinated and curious to meet him.

There we were, grinning at each other, and as the last people left, Rinpoche gave a gentle slap on the cushion next to him and beckoned for me to come sit by him. I did so, and with the help of one person, still there, who spoke pidgin English and Tibetan, and my universal language (use of hands), I managed to tell him why I was there. As soon as I introduced myself and told him I was there to offer service if he wished, he immediately held out his wrists for me to take his pulses in acceptance of the offer. After the treatment, Rinpoche noticed some improvement and asked me to return the next day. The next day became every day. In the morning I would treat many Tibetans in the village, and in the afternoon I would go up the mountainside to see Yeshe Dorje. During this period we had some wonderful talks. He was fascinated with my medical gadgets and lasers, and there was much laughter.

One day he was in a very serious mood. He told me it was his responsibility to turn his one-room hut and one-room temple into a proper monastery, representing his particular spiritual practice which dates back to the Fifth Dalai Lama. In fact His Holiness the Dalai Lama had requested this. It was then that I spontaneously suggested we write the story of his life. This would help the monastery to become better known. At the same time, the simple and moving historical account of one man's convictions and dedication to religion would be multidimensional enough to reach many people. The general public, knowing little or nothing of the Tibetans, could learn of their spiritual tradition and fascinating culture. Also, within this simple form, serious Dharma students could find great teachings. He was very excited and pleased with the idea. He was feeling very much better from the treatments and so we started at once.

I found one translator who knew a little English (the only person available to me at the time), and so, after working in the mornings with Dr. Dhonden and seeing my own patients, we met with Rinpoche every day for six weeks, working late into the night. Most of the time, I simply tape-recorded as Rinpoche told me his story and answered my questions. I wanted the information to be in as pure a form as possible.

During this time, there was an annual meeting of all the representatives (heads) of different Tibetan settlement camps throughout India and many representatives from all over the world. There was to be a big celebration at the Drama School, now known as the Tibetan Institute of the Performing Arts (T.I.P.A.), and Rinpoche told me he had been asked to stop the rain on this day. I requested to go, and he simply replied, "Of course!"

The next day I climbed up the mountain past Rinpoche's house to the Drama School, where the meeting was to be held. A tent top, about fifty feet in diameter, had been set up with chairs all around in a circle. Rinpoche began his ceremony by walking around the circumference of the tent chanting to the heavens and burning special incense. The sky was overcast and grey. There were rainclouds everywhere and thunder off in the distance. As I watched the clouds move from the center of the circle to the outside and blue start peeking through, I was amazed. Soon the entire area around the tent was flooded with sunlight and beautiful blue skies.

About noon I had to go down into the village near His Holiness the Dalai Lama's palace to treat one monk. I walked out of the circle of light, down the mountain in the rain to treat the monk. At about 2:30 I walked back up the mountain in the rain to the drama party. It was quite something to behold the circle of clear weather surrounding the tent—blue skies, white clouds, with drizzle and grey clouds everywhere else. The next day as I walked through the village, I exclaimed to this one and that one how I had been with Yeshe Dorje the day before when he had stopped the rain all day! Not one person was surprised.

I realize that, for some, the life of Yeshe Dorje Rinpoche will be a fantastic story, hard to believe. As we limit our thinking, so do we restrict ourselves from discovering new truths and experiencing the totality of possibilities.

On New Year's Day, 1985, about six months after returning home to the United States, I met Professor Karen Blanc. Soon after, we began the work of writing this book.

Dr. Marsha Woolf, McLeod Ganj, India
March, 1992

PREFACE - Part II

On New Year's Day, 1985, I received a telephone call from Dr. Marsha Woolf, telling me she was in New York City. We had been speaking over the telephone since November after I had met and heard the great Tibetan Buddhist monk–physician, Dr. Yeshi Dhonden. Since it was a holiday, Dr. Woolf invited me for lunch at the East Side apartment where she was staying.

When I first met her, I felt like I was pulled out of time, suspended in another world. It was an exquisite world of beauty that seemed thousands of years old, far from my modern world of New York City. Her face seemed ageless. I listened, fascinated, as this physician told me of her travels and work in India, China, Tibet, Peru, and Europe. Her commitment to humanity touched my heart and I was moved in the deepest part of my being.

In the following months, as our friendship grew, I visited her home in Providence, Rhode Island. She showed me pictures of Yeshe Dorje Rinpoche and permitted me to listen to tapes of her personal interviews with him. When I listened to the story of his

Thomas Merton, Trappist contemplative monk, 1915-1968, wrote about sixty books and numerous articles and essays. He was perhaps the best known and most widely–read monk of all times. His autobiography, *Seven Story Mountain,* became a best seller, selling more than 600,000 copies during its first year of publication—more than any other American piece of non–fiction in 1945.

life and his teachings, I knew in my heart that he was one of God's great ones.

During my summers in college, I had lived and worked at a Christian convent where I attended classes on the scriptures, the religious life, and theology. I received spiritual direction under the sisters who introduced me to the writings of great Christian mystics such as the Desert Fathers, St. Teresa of Avila, St. Therese of Lisieux, St. Augustine, and St. John of the Cross. In the prayer–filled atmosphere of the convent, nurtured by daily mass and the Divine Office, I read all the books written by the Trappist contemplative, Thomas Merton; I considered myself his spiritual daughter.

In 1978 and 1981, I traveled to India, where I studied prayer, meditation, Eastern philosophy, and comparative religions under the guidance of Sri Sathya Sai Baba of Puttaparthi. Upon my return I accompanied my spiritual teacher, Hilda Charlton, to the Cathedral of St. John the Divine, where I heard and met His Holiness the Dalai Lama, received his blessing, and first heard of the Tibetan holocaust.

It was from the great traditions of mysticism and contemplative prayer in Christianity, Hinduism, the tantric yoga of the caves of the Himalayas, and the raja yoga of the jungles and forests in India that I listened to Yeshe Dorje Rinpoche. Here is a genuine yogi, a genuine spiritual man, who has great powers and a great story, I thought. When Dr. Woolf, therefore, asked me to co–author this book with her, I responded with heartfelt enthusiasm for I knew Rinpoche's life and teachings reflected the very purest tantra yoga of Tibetan Buddhism.

In writing this book with her, we had to research the Chinese invasion of Tibet in order to write our commentaries. We read that the Chinese People's Army destroyed over six thousand monasteries in Tibet and tortured and killed ninety percent of the monks and nuns. As citizens of this planet, we were shocked and outraged at what happened to the Tibetan people and their culture.

May this book be our humble effort as two human beings to bring the very best of Tibetan Buddhist spirituality to the world. May the truths of this tantric yoga of the caves and of the monasteries of ancient Tibet forever remain alive and vibrant in the minds and hearts of people.

Thank you, His Holiness the Dalai Lama, Yeshe Dorje Rinpoche, and Dr. Marsha Woolf, for allowing me to be part of writing and compiling this book. This book is written for God and in honor of the Tibetan people. It is also my hope that it will contribute to Thomas Merton's dream of fostering increased understanding and shared knowledge among the great monastic traditions and religions of the East and West.

Professor Karen Blanc
New York City
April, 1992

PROLOGUE

Approximately eighteen hours north of Delhi, in the mountains, lies the village of McLeod Ganj, upper Dharamsala. Situated at the lower edge of the Dhauladhar Mountain Range and overlooking the Kangra Valley is Dharamsala, a hill station established by the British Raj in the mid-nineteenth century. The British government abandoned India in 1947.

It was not until 1959 that His Holiness the Dalai Lama, the spiritual and temporal leader of Tibet, and his people fled Tibet and were given political sanctuary by the Indian government. He established the Tibetan government-in-exile in Dharamsala. Today there are approximately 110,000 refugees living throughout India, mostly in Tibetan refugee camps.

• • •

The narrative portion of this story is as told by Yeshe Dorje Rinpoche to Dr. Marsha Woolf, using transcriptions of extensive interview tapes. All other commentaries are written by the authors.

Photo courtesy of
The Library of Tibetan
Works and Archives,
Dharamsala, India

Chapter One:
THE EARLY YEARS

When His Holiness the Dalai Lama was forced to leave Tibet in 1959 because of the Chinese invasion, he established his government–in–exile in Dharamsala. The Dalai Lama requested Yeshe Dorje *Rinpoche* to come to Dharamsala to start a *Nyingma* monastery, one of the four Tibetan Buddhist sects, so that all sects would be represented there. Thus, Dharramsala became the capital of Tibet-in–exile, and the Dalai Lama is the spiritual and temporal leader of all Tibet. Tibetan Buddhists believe that the current Dalai Lama has been reincarnated fourteen times to carry on the tradition of Tibetan Buddhism.

Fearful of Western imperialism and needing Tibet's strategically invaluable land in case of trouble with Russia or India, the People's Republic of China sought to annex Tibet—in their view, to "liberate" Tibet. The aim of the Chinese Communist Party was to merge Tibet with the Motherland, both politically and culturally. To the Tibetans, however, liberation meant spiritual freedom—the freedom of the soul from the body and from the sufferings of earthly life. Thus, in this respect, the philosophies of the Tibetans and the Chinese were antithetical to one another.

Rinpoche means "precious one" and is a title given to incarnated and highly–realized beings.

Nyingma is the oldest of four Tibetan Buddhist sects. The others are Kagyu, Gelug, and Sakya.

So the Chinese Communist Party's modern army came to the land of beautiful snow–capped mountains and thousands of monasteries. By the summer of 1949, the army had invaded Amdo and had begun to approach the borders of Kham in eastern Tibet. Having experienced its own inner political conflicts as well as massive destruction by one of the world's five most devastating earthquakes, Tibet was particularly vulnerable to impending occupation by the Chinese.

The Chinese Peoples Liberation Army (PLA) entered Kham in 1950. By the end of 1951, 20,000 troops (almost half of the city's population) were occupying Lhasa, the capital of Tibet, a country that had virtually no standing army. On two occasions the Tibetan government was forced to "loan" the Chinese 2,000 tons of grain, thereby destroying the economic structure of the city and causing great famine and poverty among the Tibetan people. The Tibetans revolted, marking the beginning of the resistance group called The Defender of the Faith.

In 1955, the PLA workers infiltrated the countryside and villages of the Kham and Amdo regions. Promoting their programs, which they called "Democratic Reforms," they confiscated private property from the Tibetans and set up communes. Not only did the Chinese force Tibetans at gunpoint to accept the program and philosophy, they took Tibetan children from their parents and made them wards of the state. Public executions at this time were the mere precursor of the holocaust that followed.

From the beginning of the Chinese invasion, His Holiness the Dalai Lama had made countless efforts, including personal diplomatic visits to China and India, to resolve differences with the Chinese government and to gain support from the outside world. His efforts were not successful. In 1957, over 150,000 Chinese troops, supported by bombers and tanks, attacked Kham, devastating villages that housed primarily women, children and the elderly.

Countless public executions, as well as extermination of entire villages, instilled fear in the remaining populace. Children were coerced into shooting their parents and were beaten or tortured if they refused. Monks were forced to endure public sex with nuns and other humiliations. Tibetans were imprisoned without trials; 173,221 were placed in prison camps. Additionally, 342,970 suffered from starvation.

Other forms of torture included hanging people by their fingers and pouring boiling water on others. Many Tibetan men were forced to be sterilized. Eyes, mouths, tongues and genitalia were burned. People were beheaded, dismembered, burned, and buried alive.

Approximately 1.2 million Tibetans, including about ninety percent of their monks, were slaughtered by the Chinese. Six thousand monasteries were destroyed, including eighty percent of Tibetan religious items such as scriptures, paintings, and artifacts. While the Tibetans–in–exile have established a thriving government–in–exile at Dharamsala, Tibet is not formally recognized by any country, including India.

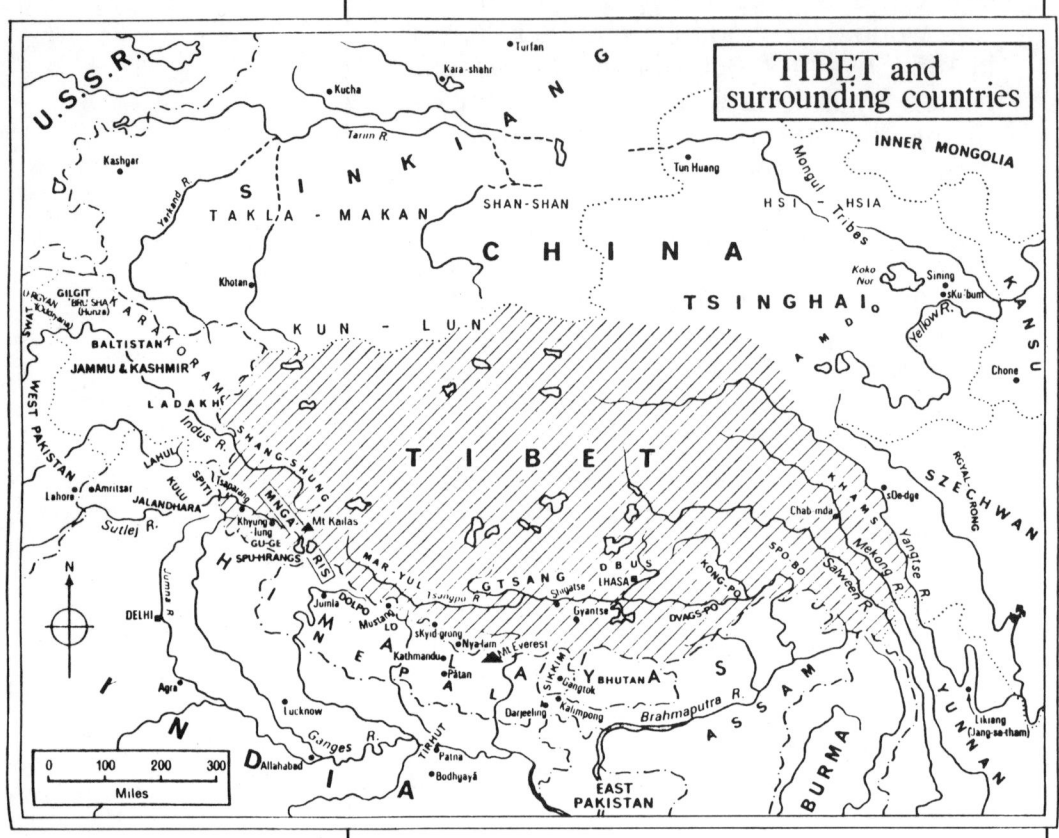

From *A Cultural History of Tibet* by David Shellgrove and Hugh Richardson; Prajna Press, 1980.
For a current political map of India, refer to page 101 of this book.

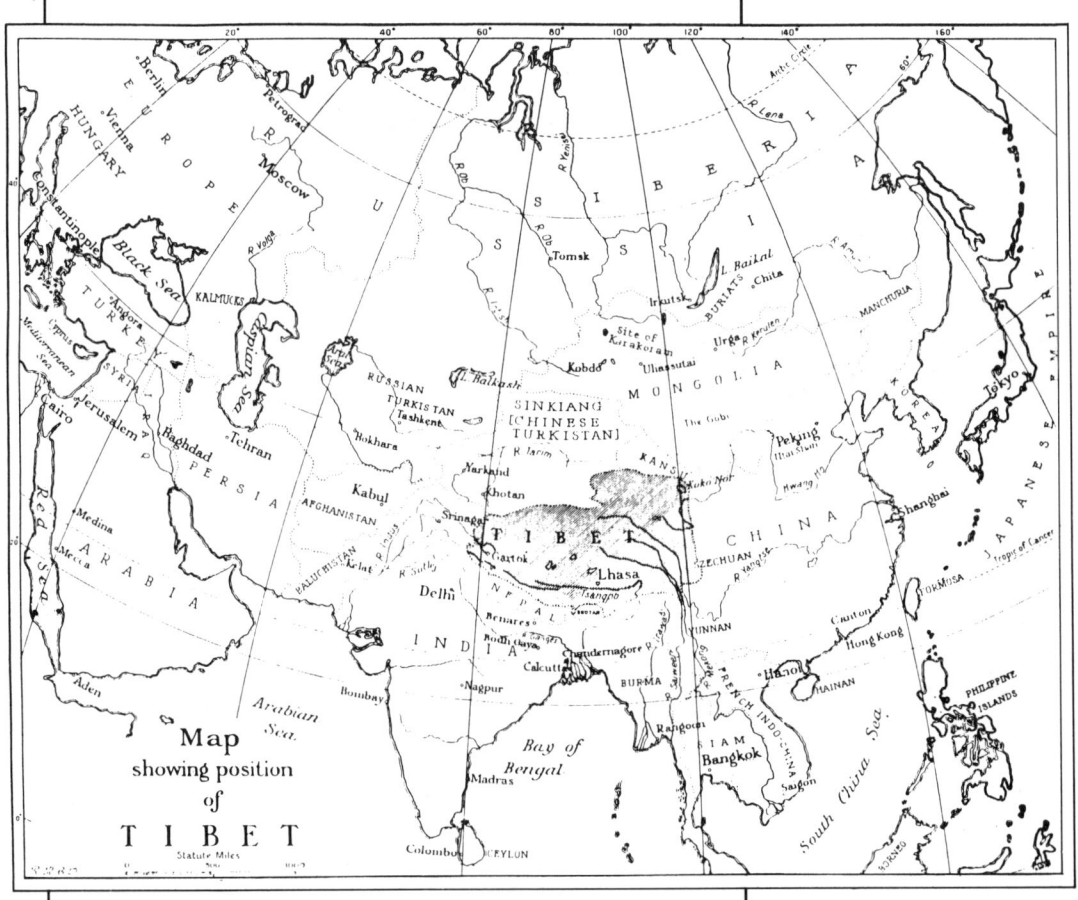

From *The Religion of Tibet* by Sir Charles Bell; Oxford University Press, 1931, 1968, 1970.
For a current political map of India, refer to page 101 of this book.

• • • • •

Yeshe Dorje Rinpoche came from a centuries-long father–to–son lineage of weather controllers. Moreover, Migyur Dorje, from whom Yeshe Dorje descended directly, was a contemporary of the Fifth Dalai Lama. He was the abbot of the monastery from which Yeshe Dorje continued teaching many years later. Yeshe Dorje was an especially gifted Rinpoche: he traveled to Tibetan settlement camps throughout India in order to make or stop the rain.

The first official recognition that Yeshe Dorje was a gifted spiritual being happened at the age of five when he was out in the mountains with his father and older brother one day. The young boy got lost, and his father, who was a famous medical astrologer, calculated where he was. The father was surprised to find Yeshe Dorje in a cave behind a mountain that was considered impossible for a young boy to climb in such a short time.

Planning to tie a rope around the boy, Yeshe Dorje's brother lowered himself down from the top of the mountain on a rope (shown in the illustration on the facing page). Just as his brother approached, the noise frightened Yeshe Dorje so much that he stepped out onto the ledge and was about to jump. His brother quickly caught him, and they were raised to safety. After the incident, Yeshe Dorje remembers sitting at home on his father's lap with many *shabten* going on in the house. So then, at the age of five, after that happening, his father consulted high lamas to determine

<u>Shabten</u> are rituals or prayer ceremonies; also called *pooja*.

Drawing by Karma Norbu

whether he was a special yogi, a *tulku*. Many high lamas came and gave him special tests, all of which he passed. Then they had a celebration of the incarnation.

Tulku is a recognized reincarnated being.

• • • • •

Now, Yeshe Dorje Rinpoche tells his story:

I was born the first month and fifteenth day of the fire tiger year, in 1926, in Markham, which is in the Kham area of eastern Tibet. There were two brothers and one sister in my family. My father's name was Orygan Dorje, and my mother's name was Sonam Dolma. They were also from the Kham area.

My family is called Dompatsang. They come from Lharong, a place in Markham. Their lineage is passed through the family. If there are two sons, one can become a monk. If there is only one son, he is not allowed to become a monk because he has to preserve the lineage. My whole family belongs to the lineage.

My eldest brother became a monk, and because I was recognized as the *tulku* and former head of the of the Do–Nag Choling Monastery, it was my responsibility to hold the throne as I had done in my previous incarnation. My other brother stayed with my parents to do the family work.

My family has stopped hail for centuries. This gift has been passed on from father to son. One of my spiritual fathers, Yogi Tashi, who was also a contemporary of the Fifth Dalai Lama, was a great practitioner. Actually, my immediate spiritual lineage began with him.

He was a real yogi who did not care about daily problems. He lived inside his mind. He was a highly realized being, but externally he seemed to be a very ordinary being. The government sent people to his village to collect taxes. Sometimes they used force to try to get the citizens to pay taxes. He felt the government was wrong so he said he was not going to pay.

Because he refused to pay taxes, the government sent the police to arrest him. When the police arrived, about fifty of them with guns and swords surrounded his house. Then ten police came in to search the house, where they found and bound his wife, children and other family members to pillars. Yogi Tashi was on the second story of the house where he was saying his prayers.

One man told the family to tell Yogi Tashi to come down. "First," Yogi Tashi said, "release all my children, my wife and other family members, and then one of you can come up and I will talk to you." So a few of them went up with their weapons and they yelled at him. As they told him to pay the tax, he did not say anything. He took off all his clothes except his loincloth, and he ran here and there.

He was actually performing *lung gom* and soon appeared to be flying around above the roof, as shown in the drawing on the following page. The police were very surprised and they realized he must be a great man. Bowing down and apologizing profusely, they prostrated themselves before him and were very sad. They said, "Sorry. We made a mistake" and proclaimed that he was a special yogi and should be respected.

It is said that Yogi Tashi was actually able to change into an eagle so that he could benefit some special animals and lead them into liberation. Yogi Tashi manifested in this form and delivered many beings. He gave teachings to those beings and then returned to human form. And that is how my lineage began.

Lung gom is a meditation technique utilizing the subtle internal airs or winds of the body.

Drawing by Karma Norbu

Chapter Two
IN THE MONASTERY

At the age of five, when I was recognized as a special incarnated being, I was sent to the Do–Nag Choeling Monastery in Markham, where I received special privileges. I studied reading and writing and memorized all the prayers. During that time, I also finished my examination of memorization of all the prayers.

While I was in the monastery I memorized texts and learned how to do rituals and shabten. At the age of fifteen I took and passed the examination of memorization. My teacher's name was Pema Dorje.

As a child, I liked to play many games and tricks on people for fun. I even teased the monks. When I was fifteen, my teacher was very strict, which greatly scared me. I could not remember my studies because I was so scared. This made me very slow at memorizing.

My teacher was thinking of leaving the monastery for Lhasa. The reason, I was to learn later, was because of me. One night, I had a dream in which a *khadroma* appeared and admonished me for not memorizing and told me to take

Khadroma is a female angelic deity; also called *dakini*.

care with my studies. When I woke up, I looked at my texts and tried to memorize them. I found that it was quite easy.

I memorized 180 pages in one month. Then I had another dream in which the *khadroma* told me that I was ready to take the examination. I asked my teacher if I could take the examination. He could not believe that I was ready. But I said that I was and he granted the examination.

This type of examination is special because the abbot or teacher can pick any line in the text and the student must immediately recite the lines that follow in the text by memory. This is one way of giving an examination to a student.

During a special *shabten* my teacher looked at me with a serious face. He had a beard and looked frightening. He thought I probably had not passed the examination. Usually after the *shabten*, I played with the other monks, but on that day I went straight home. The teacher also came along and stood right in my house, where there were two adjoining rooms. My teacher stayed in one room, and I stayed in the other. He prostrated in front of me.

Usually when a teacher has to punish an incarnated being, he has to prostrate three times. I thought I was going to be punished, but my teacher was very happy and was crying. He said, "I am very sorry because I always thought you were very stupid; but now I regret it very much and from now on, I will teach you very nicely."

My teacher told me that because I had not been careful with my studies, he had lost hope in me. If I had not passed the examination, his reputation would have been affected and he would have been ashamed. He had been planning to leave the monastery and go to Lhasa. He had even purchased horses for the journey. Now that I had passed the examination, he was disclosing all these things to me. He had changed his mind about leaving and decided to stay to teach me. He collected all of his horses and sold them.

From that time onward, people in the monasteries started to respect me. They showed great affection to me and came to see me on special days. Even high lamas began visiting me. Relatives from far away started to come with gifts. I stayed four years, during which time there were many celebrations for passing the examination.

One day I met three Dregung Kagyue *chodpas* who were returning from a long pilgrimage to Eastern Tibet and China. I was deeply moved by them. I told myself, "If you want to become a practitioner, you should take their example." That was a turning point in my religious life. Then and there I decided to become something like them.

Chodpas are practitioners of exorcism.

Soon after, I prepared to leave the monastery because I thought I should learn to depend upon myself instead of others. In the monastery most people offered things, and these donations helped the monasteries to survive and grow. I thought this method of living was a way of accumulating things, and I thought it would better if I earned and spent my own money rather than spending the money of others. I did not want to accumulate much nonvirtue.

Also, in the monastery, you do what the others do and not what you want to do. So you do not get the chance to think separately for yourself. In the monastery, I had depended all of my life on the offerings of other people, but I had not done anything for them. In my country, when people die they make offerings to the high lama so that he will send some help to the spirit of the person who has died. I thought to myself that, until this time, I have had no powers. I had just accumulated the offerings of other people. It seemed to me I had accumulated a lot of nonvirtue because I could do nothing for others without such powers.

Lord Buddha said, "To practice the *dharma* perfectly you should disown all material things. We should not be attached to worldly things." I believed there was much wealth in the monastery. If I stayed there I would live off this wealth and not truly practice the *dharma*. Lord Buddha also said, "If you want to

Dharma is a common name for all religions or any love or compassion traditions.

do the real practice of the *dharma,* you should go away from your relatives and your belongings. You must go out into the world that you have never seen, which is not near family. You should disown your wealth, everything." It is the teaching of the Lord Buddha that one should go for a distance that would take three years of just walking to find. After making this walk for three years, there will be a place to practice real *dharma,* and then you should not go on walking. You should stay there. If you are a common person, you should live at least three days walking distance from your family, relatives, and children.

I left the monastery secretly. I ran away. I had five horses with me and some religious texts and things important to me. It was not really very much. In the daytime I stayed by the hillside and at night kept moving. Then I reached Kongpo. At that time I met one person who said if I went to Lhasa I would have a chance of having an audience with the Dalai Lama. The man said if I wanted to go with him he knew the whole route and it would be very nice to travel together, and so we went to Lhasa. This trip took months.

When I reached Lhasa, I tried to see the Dalai Lama but did not get the opportunity. I continued on my journey and found a teacher. His name was Kogyon Rinpoche and he was a very old man. He told me how he got his name. Most of us, these days, get our names by going to the Dalai Lama. When my teacher was very young, his parents died, and so, being orphaned, when he was growing up he had few clothes. He thought he should have clothes of leather because they would last longer. In Tibetan *kowa* means leather and *gyon* means wear, the Rinpoche who wears leather. That was how he got his name. Kogyon Rinpoche was my first really important teacher.

I studied with my teacher for more than two years. You can study with many different lamas, but if you have one that is close to you then you will learn more from that one than by just running around seeing different lamas and not getting the essence of what they have to say. The essence of his teachings was on meditation, on voidness, on emptiness. I did not learn how to do *shabten* or to perform rituals that were the outer forms of religion. I just learned the inner essence, the emptiness of all things. He told me that if I were to do *dharma* practice successfully, there was a hope we would meet again someday. After that, he died.

Until now, I have not met him again. My teacher said if I do the *dharma* practice successfully, I will not be of the earth, so if I do this there will be every opportunity that we will be meeting in paradise—pure land—where there is no dying, no birth: the world of great bliss.

When my teacher died, instead of dying in the normal way and leaving a body behind, all that remained of him was his hair, his fingernails, and toenails. The rest of him dissolved into rainbow dust.

When I was twenty–two I met my Nyingma teacher, His Holiness Dudjom Rinpoche, head of the Nyingmapa lineage. There were many teachings, initiations, both written and oral instructions on numerous texts, and meditation practices. I studied *Rinchen Terzod* (which contains 116 volumes) along with two other major Nyingmapa texts: the *Nyingma Gyudbum* and *Kama*.

His Holiness Dudjom Rinpoche
Photo courtesy of Zilnon Kagyeling Monastery

Chapter Three
MEDITATION AND RETREAT

There is an old story in India about a king who banished another king. The banished king was named Trimed Kunden. He went to Tibet and decided to stay in Kongpo in order to undergo a long retreat at the notorious demon-infested cave, filled with evil spirits. This cave was in a small mountain called Dudri Hashang Kem Kem Ri. *Dudri* means hill of demons. I decided to go to that place for a retreat, to meditate.

There I meditated for three years, three months, and three days. I was twenty–seven years old. This was my first long retreat for which the initiations and transmissions were granted by His Holiness Dudjom Rinpoche, and teachings in the retreat were given by Venerable Doring Tulku. During the meditation I felt as if my mind was wandering. Although I had been given instructions on very important subjects, I started thinking about other things. I was thinking about my relatives and teachers, imagining they were there with me.

Many Demons Cave
Drawing by Karma Norbu

In my imagination, a person appeared in front of me announcing that he was my elder brother and that he had come with the news that my father had died and I should immediately go home. The man had a white horse. I started to get on the horse to go and then realized the nature of impermanence. I thought I should not go because if my father had died, he had died, and nothing could be done now. The negative entities do not like people doing good things, so when a person briefly stops doing good things, the devils try to disturb the person by interfering with his feelings.

I thought about the fact that every person dies. Then I realized my meditation should not be disturbed and I should not be distracted by worldly things. I prayed to my teacher for his blessing. It is quite common for a person who has stopped meditation to have such experiences.

After that incident about news of my father's death, I continued meditating in my room once again. After quite sometime, I had another illusion. I saw meats all around the room, hanging to dry. There were all kinds of foodstuffs, so there was a great variety to choose from. They looked delicious, and I thought I would eat some. So I took out my knife and cut one piece of meat. I was about to eat it and suddenly thought that I should not eat this piece of meat. I should give it for an offering.

Immediately I saw blood running on my leg and noticed that there was no meat in the room. I had cut my own flesh. One of the other disciples of Rinpoche noticed what I had done and went immediately to my teacher, who came right away. I could not stand so he picked me up and placed me on the veranda. He washed all of the blood off my leg and gave me injections of medicine. He told me I should stay in the retreat and finish it. I stayed for the final seven nights and seven days.

Because during the retreat I was not supposed to eat much, when my teacher gave me three pills to take, I thought I was going to faint. One day there was sunshine, and I went outside thinking I was breaking the retreat, that only a few days had passed. In fact I had been in retreat two weeks. He told me I had finished the retreat and should not worry.

The cut I had made had been so deep it went to the bone. When he tried to remove the bandage, he could not open it and so they soaked it. Then they opened the bandage a little at a time, and my wound was completely healed. There was no pus or infection. It had only been one week. Even though the wound was healed, I still could not walk properly for one year. In retreat, one is not supposed to keep any knife or weapon around. There are many cases similar to this and that is why there is this rule.

After that I went to His Holiness Dudjom Rinpoche's monastery, Lamaling Monastery, where there were five hundred nuns and monks doing a retreat. I joined the retreat and was praised for the high level of realization and total emptiness I had reached by successfully completing the previous three–year, three–month, three–day retreat. A ceremonial white scarf was presented to me. The sponsor of the retreat was Sangay Dorje, a very rich and important person in this area.

My teacher Dudjom Rinpoche asked me to go to his house. He told me he wanted me to do a special retreat. He had already sent word to Sangay Dorje, who consented to be my sponsor. On my way to this retreat, I stopped at the sponsor's house to do *shabten* for him and his family. They gave me food and supplies.

My retreat was in a very strange place. It was strange because it went in two directions. In the middle was a small, rocky hill, near a very rough river. It was a frightening place where no one had ever been able to stay in a long retreat. In fact, many aspirants had died trying. Demons were imprisoned there, so it was a very hostile place. I stayed there one month and a half. In the beginning I faced a lot of problems and was afraid. I was alone. After awhile my fear subsided and no illusions appeared to me. My mind was clear and I was able to do my retreat quietly and successfully.

When I finished, I stopped again at the sponsor's house. He was very happy to see me and congratulated me for successfully completing this retreat and offered me two mules. One mule was loaded with rice, the other with butter. He told me that because I had completed this retreat, I was now free of any demons from that place.

A few years later I decided to go to a place called Lungta Jemai Chodten (sand *stupa* place). I went to visit the cave that Guru Padmasambhava had meditated in. It was a sandy terrain, with a very hot climate and little water. It is said that one day, as Guru Padmasambhava was outside the cave, it was so hot that his nose started to bleed and some of the blood dropped into the sand. This sand automatically formed into a huge *stupa* with his blood in the very center. My plan was to meditate in that cave for three years, three months, and three days.

Stupa is a funerary mount or monument serving as a Buddhist shrine.

While I was meditating in that place, there was a man staying with me as my servant. At one point he told me that the firewood was used up and that we had no more. This was at the end of the first year. I told him we would just use whatever we had and that we would be all right by the next day. When he woke up in the morning, he saw a huge pile of firewood had been placed before the cave. He asked me what we should do with it, and I told him that we should use it and not to worry. Later that day my servant found the flesh of many animals which had been placed in front of the cave. I suggested it was a present for us and we should eat it.

From that time onward, we were given firewood and the flesh of animals. About four months later my servant saw a dead body of a small child laying outside the cave. As cremation is the customary way of disposing of the dead, we took the body to appropriately burn it. While we were walking on the road, we saw a huge footprint. My attendant was horrified.

We found out that there was a three-member family of *yetis*: a mother, father, and son. During that second year when I was meditating in the cave, these *yetis* brought firewood from the jungle. They also brought the flesh of different kinds of animals, left them just outside the cave, and vanished. As I said before, my attendant was very frightened. He told me that I could meditate in any other

Yetis are primitive snowpeople.

place and he would come there and serve me, but pleaded that I leave this place. He said he was very nervous. I told him he was free to go but that I was staying. So he left. I did not see him until in Dharamsala many years later.

The *yetis* continued to supply me with firewood and food for the remainder of the second year. After that, when all the people in the surrounding area came to know that the *yetis* were feeding me, they were so surprised that everyone came to see me. They served me and sought my blessings. This greatly disturbed my meditation, so I left that place unable to complete the three–years, three–months, and three–days retreat.

Yeshe Dorje Rinpoche
Dharamsala, 1983
Photo by Dr. Marsha Woolf

Chapter Four:
JOURNEY AND RAINMAKING

After the experience with the *yetis*, I went to Tsari, which is situated in the hills where there are many religious places to which people go on pilgrimage. There were three routes leading through nine different hills which all form the lines of a great *mandala*. I chose the middle route, which takes eleven or twelve days to travel. This was the route for the monastery of Sangag Choeling. There were many bandits and hostile tribes along this road. They carried weapons and used spears and bows. They robbed people of their grain, foodstuffs, and money in order to let them pass. They also killed many people.

When I reached the monastery, they were having a long-life ritual. There were many people and a great celebration. People were bringing offerings for Guru Rinpoche. The celebration was in honor of the completion of a statue of Guru Rinpoche that was two stories high. I stayed to receive initiation from a special lama and left.

Mandala is a Hindu or Buddhist graphic symbol of the universe, specifically a circle enclosing a square with a deity on each side.

Powa is transference of consciousness.

Chod here means severing or cutting of the ego; also means exorcism in Nyingma tradition.

Tsampa is roasted barley flour, the staple food of Tibet.

From there I went to Lhodrak, which is in the southern part of Tibet. There I received the *powa* teaching from a lama named Namkhai Nyingpo. Teachings concerning the *chod* practice were also received from Yeshe Nyingpo.

I did a retreat there for three months in the cave which belonged to Karma Wangzin. Soon my food supply ran out and I had to stop my meditation. I visited a town, Drong Ongpo, which was very near the cave, and asked one family to give me some *tsampa*. That family told me that they did not have any surplus provisions and to ask another family. So I asked another family nearby. They told me that they knew I was a very great lama and that the village was having problems with shortages of food because there had been a drought for a very long time. They asked me to do a rain ritual and told me that afterwards I could have supper. This was the first time that I made rain.

I continued to make rain for three days in that village. I was on the banks of a very big river. On the other side of the river there was a district called Singe Dzong. *Dzong* means district and the name of the district is *Singe,* which means Snow Lion. The people of that district heard that there was a lama who could make rain in the village across the river. They needed rain in their district also and so they sent for me to come to their place. When someone came for me,

I explained that I was a yogi and it was my intention to meditate on the hillside in the cave and I had just come out for foodstuffs. A little while later many people came collectively and asked me if I would please help their district and said that they would do anything for me if I would help. So I had to go to that place.

When I reached that district, I saw the head magistrate. He was also a very religious person and received me with a warm welcome. In order to make rain, it is necessary to have water nearby, and so I knew I could make rain in this place because of the river. I asked many of the people in the district to bring all of the offerings, articles, and things necessary for the rainmaking ritual. A tent was pitched for me near the water. Many of the district people came to witness how I made the rain. The district magistrate also had a tent pitched so that he could observe me. I was warned by some people that I had better be successful because this district magistrate could be a very cruel man and could punish me. So I was a bit nervous and uneasy as I started doing *shabten* and making offerings.

At my first attempt I could not make rain and got angry at myself because I really wanted to help these people. So I meditated and transformed myself into Troma Nagmo, the black *dakini* which is my principal *yidam* or meditational deity for all my practices including weather controlling. Then I called on the God of

Dakini is a female angelic deity; also called *khadroma*.

Yeshe Dorje Rinpoche performing weather-controlling ceremony
Photo by Philip Hemley

Water, Migon Karp. He is like the king, the owner, or master of the water. I shook the pond with a stick, briskly, over and over, calling on the King of Water to help. All at once a big white rock came out from the water. At first I was startled. Then I realized that now I was going to make the rain. I continued the ritual, made offerings, and saw a black cloud form directly over my tent. That cloud started to grow gradually, becoming bigger and bigger. Soon there was the sound of thunder.

It rained and hailed heavily on both the villages, extending to the entire district. I told the district magistrate that I wanted to go back to my meditation. I had made the rain they wanted, so then I was going to leave. The magistrate told me I should make rain for at least a week because the lands and villages needed rain very badly. So I agreed. I kept the ritual going, and it rained the entire time. During the seven days, I stayed in the house of the district magistrate. Then I told the magistrate that I could not make rain anymore and I wanted to leave that place and go back to where I had been meditating previously. He told me that this was all right and arranged for horses for my departure.

Many of the people in the village had come to me while I was there, asking me to make special *shabten* for them. I stayed for a while but then decided to continue with my meditation and left quietly one morning.

After traveling some time, I came to Lhodrak Sengkhar Guthok, which means a temple of nine stories, and then to a place called Drumtso Pemaling. *Drumtso* is the name of a lake and *Pemaling* means lotus valley. In that place there is a monastery of Guru Padmasambhava. After visiting these monasteries and lakes, I went off to the hill to a cave in which Guru Padmasambhava had meditated. I meditated there for six months.

My food supplies were finished and so I had to leave. After visiting the Lhalung Monastery, I proceeded on to a small village. There I got a very good sponsor who gave me clothes and food. I continued my journey to a place called Phuma Chanthang. I meditated in a cave at the top of a hill called Nyingri, meaning heart–shaped hill, for three years, three months, and three days.

It was quite a difficult place to meditate because the water was at the bottom of the hill. I had to continually go up and down to get the water. Finally, I dug a small hole in the ground beside my cave and prayed that, if I had the good karma of meditating in this cave, the gods would give me water. I covered the hole and went back to my cave. The next morning I went to that place and looked in the hole and found it was filled with water. It was not much water, but it was just enough to fill the vessel that I had with me at that time. I gathered the water and offered it to the gods. Then I used

*Nyingri Cave, or heart-shaped cave, where Rinpoche did a three-year retreat
Drawing by Karma Norbu*

the water for cooking purposes. The next day, I found the hole was filled with water once again. From that day on, I did not face any problems and was able to meditate for the full three years, three months, and three days.

After finishing the meditation, I stayed in that cave for one more month. The people of the village had come to know that there was a lama on the hill where there was no possibility of getting water. They were surprised that I was able to stay there and started to come to visit me and bring offerings. Many people asked me to do *shabten* for them. And, after awhile, I left. To this day people from that region, who now live in India, call me Nyingri Lama.

During the winter I arrived in a beautiful place where there was a lake called Phuma Yumtsho. In the middle of the lake was an island with a hill on it. The only possibility of getting to this island was to walk across the ice. I gathered foodstuffs and clothes that I needed and walked on the ice across the lake to the island. There was a cave in the hill. I planned to meditate there for three years, three months, and three days.

After meditating for a year, I ran into some problems. My matches were finished so I could not have any fire, hot foods, or liquids, and it was very cold. I could not leave because there was no ice. After a month of hardship, I had a dream very early in the morning. It was not exactly a dream. I saw a lady standing in my cave. She appeared to me. She said, "Today you should go to the monastery called Thue Gompa." Then she vanished.

I woke up and did not see the lady anywhere in the cave. And I did not know if it was a dream or real. I thought since it was not winter that if I crossed over this lake I might drown. But the lady seemed so real that I thought that it was a clear sign for me to leave. So I did a *shabten*, made offerings, and prayed to my guru. It was around three in the morning. As I walked out from the cave, I looked at the lake and saw a small pathway that looked like shiny, white cloth. It led from my cave across the water to the opposite bank.

I left the cave and by the time I reached the opposite bank, the sun was about to rise. I went to the monastery and was taken into the abbot's house, to his room,

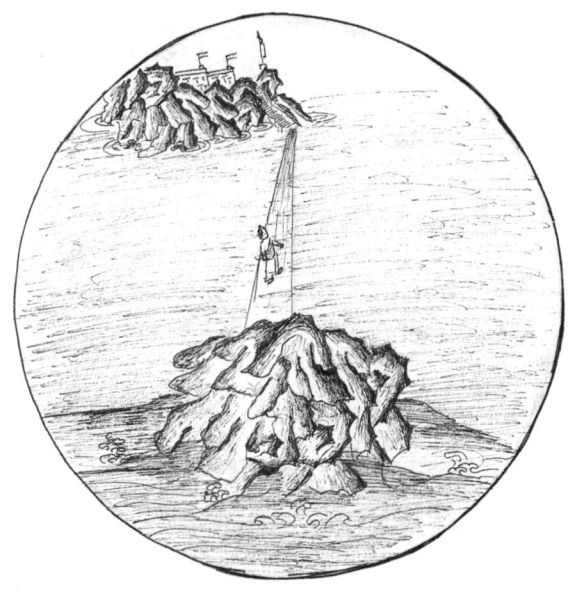

*Ice path leading
Rinpoche to safety*
Drawing by Karma Norbu

where they offered me a plate of hot porridge. This was my first hot food in a month. After finishing my food, I asked if they could please arrange to bring me some matches so that I could go back and complete my meditation. I had left my shoes at the bank of the lake because to reach the temple I had to climb a hill, and my shoes were very wet. I told everyone I had to go back after my shoes, but people insisted I stay.

   A few minutes later, the abbot was drying my shoes on the sand outside the monastery. He set the shoes down in the sun and started prostrating himself before me. I asked him why he was making prostrations. He said that it was quite surprising to him that I had crossed this lake. He pointed to the lake and the thin path of ice upon which I had traveled. I explained I had left the cave at three in the morning and could not see clearly in the night. The ice shone like a white cloth. I did not know it was ice. I just knew it was like a path of light. And as we looked, the ice was almost melted. Everyone at the monastery was very surprised because this was not usually a period when there was ice on the lake. They were amazed that I had crossed the lake on the ice pathway.

I could not return to the cave because there was no ice, so I stayed at that monastery for a month and a half, during which I was treated very nicely. When it was winter, I went back to the cave to complete the retreat. I stayed there three years, three months, and three days. After I finished, I rested in the cave for fifteen days more and then left. It was winter and I could walk on the ice to the other side. I stayed with the family that had sponsored me for a short period. Many people had heard that I was the person that had meditated in the island cave. They came asking for *shabten* and blessings at all hours of the day and night. I could not sleep properly, and it was also very difficult for me to do my regular morning prayers. I got sick. I had trouble with my back because I had been sitting for three years on hard, cold rock. After staying with that family for a short time, I decided to leave and proceed toward Lhasa.

Chapter Five:

TRANSMUTATION, THE CHINESE INVASION, AND EXILE FROM TIBET

I stopped in Tsethang on the way to Lhasa. I stayed with a family there who agreed to be a sponsor. One day I was in a field when a woman came running towards me. She told me that a woman who had been lodging in her house had died, and she wanted me to perform the last rites. The lama who lived in that area had left quickly to avoid doing the rites.

I went to the house and found a dead body which was about to rise. It was lying down with one leg up. As I started doing the rites, the corpse raised its other leg. This made me quite nervous. I realized if I was frightened it was because I was not concentrating. So I collected my thoughts and concentrated on the *chod* practice and the lives and deeds of great tantric practitioners. I sat on that corpse and started doing the rites and rituals.

The corpse was moving so violently trying to throw me off that it was not

Chod means exorcism in this context.

easy for me to sit. This supposedly dead body seemed to be having convulsions. Everybody in the house was very afraid of this corpse. As I sat on it, wondering what to do, I remembered that in *chod* scriptures there is a section on the transfer of consciousness. I began to recite this section to calm down the corpse and to allow consciousness to leave it.

There was a lot of blood coming out of all the orifices, which made a really gruesome sight. There was also a strong odor. The people in the house became so frightened that they left the house and locked me inside with the corpse. I shouted through the door and finally made them open the door. Meanwhile, the lama who had run away returned, offering his help.

In Tibet, at the time of death, the way in which the corpse is disposed of depends on the horoscope of the deceased. The lama makes calculations depending upon which element rules at the time of the death: air, fire, earth, or water. If it is air, the body is cut in pieces on top of a mountain and given to the vultures so that it may return to the air. This is considered a sky burial. If it is fire, the body is put on the fire to return to the fire element. If it is the earth element, the body is buried. If it is the water element, the body is cut up and thrown into the river.

In the case of this woman, her corpse was to be taken to the mountain and given to the vultures. They took the body out of the house to a mountain behind the monastery, where it was cut into pieces. I performed the ritual to call all the vultures to eat the dead body. The vultures gathered around the body; yet they did not touch it. This showed me that something was either wrong with the body or distracting the vultures. So I did special purifying rites for the body so that it might be eaten by the vultures. After finishing these rites, the vultures still did not touch the body. For this reason, I did a special ritual for the vultures. I had to recite all the invitations to the vultures 108 times as part of this ritual. Yet they still did not eat. When the vultures refuse to take dead meat, there is only one last resort. The yogi doing the ritual must take a small piece of that flesh and eat it himself. When I did this, the vultures gathered and within a very short period the vultures ate the body.

Then I returned to the house where the family of the woman and other people requested that I stay for three weeks to continue doing *shabten*. In Tibet, when someone dies, rituals must be performed for forty–nine days: at the end of every seven days for seven weeks. Within that time period, the consciousness, or soul, leaves the *bardo* either to be reborn or reincarnated within two years.

The purpose of my staying three weeks to recite prayers was to introduce the dead spirit to her deadness and to urge her to go on her way peacefully. After

Bardo is the place of transition between lifetimes—the place where one goes after death, before the next incarnation.

*Yeshe Dorje Rinpche
performing shabten*
Photo by Philip Hemley

the twenty–first day I took all the family members of the deceased for a pilgrimage to the religious places in the area, including the Yanglung Shedrak Monastery. It was a beautiful place where a lot of medicinal herbs grew. The temple was constructed in the olden days on the sand. Every year many different kinds of birds gathered there. The temple was constructed on this site because the birds had been coming for many years and it was considered to be a holy place.

The government provided food for the birds, including fruits imported from Nepal. It appeared that the birds were doing an evaluation of each other. Some seemed to be promoted, while others seemed to be punished by the other birds. And some were even killed by the others. This gathering on the sands of the temple lasted fifteen days. Instead of twenty–one days I kept doing the *shabten* for forty–nine. Then I proceeded towards Lhasa once more. The families arranged the provisions for the journey, including new garments, food, and supplies.

Then I arrived at Kongpo Demo Monastery, where there had been an earthquake. It had been completely destroyed and fifteen people had died. I knew the lama there who asked me if I would help because some of the corpses were rising. I told him I thought we should not do this alone and so we got another Rinpoche and his seven disciples to come with us to that place. One corpse had a raised hand, and its other one was on the ground ready to push its body up. We decided since there were so many corpses, it was better to do a common ritual for all of them. There was a cemetery nearby. As we were conducting the ritual, another part of the building collapsed on some of the dead bodies. There was one corpse that was standing. I went over and hit it with my thighbone trumpet. This was to activate a transference of consciousness and to communicate to the corpse that it was dead. Soon the corpse was lying down like a dead body.

Then I stopped at another monastery. The abbot requested that I stop the hail and strong rains because the weather had been very bad there. I did what he asked and many people in the area requested me to do *shabtens*. All the offerings that were made to me were donated to the monastery. During this time, the early 1950s, we would hear about the Chinese coming into Tibet.

As I proceeded toward Lhasa, I had to cross Kyichu River and a big, sandy desert before Samye. I met some people who had just been to Lhasa. They had been robbed of everything and were left with nothing to eat, so they were crying and asking me to help. I gave them all the garments and clothes of the dead woman back in Tsethang.

Later I met a pilgrim and we decided to travel together for a while. As we came to the top of a pass called Kongpo Ngarla, between Kongpo and Dakpo, we saw a man there with his sword drawn. Then another man came along, and they were playfully swinging their swords. When they saw us, they signaled to each other, and before we knew it, we were surrounded by seven men with their swords drawn. My friend had a sword and I had a stick.

The men asked me where I was going. I told them that we were going to Lhasa. Then they asked me what my business was and if I had anything to sell. We said that we had nothing. Then one robber tried to pull my friend from his horse. My friend, in turn, tried to grab the robber's sword. When the robber tried to hit my friend with the sword, my friend cut the robber's ear. Both got very angry and there was a big fight. One robber was about to cut my friend's throat with a knife. I thwarted his move by hitting him with a stick, but another robber shot me with a pistol.

My *gau* that I was wearing under my clothes protected me and diverted the bullet. During the fight some of the robber's blood got on my hand, even though I was wearing a protection box with many precious things in it. Since I got blood on my hand, it was a sign to me that I would be hurt. I did get hurt by the bullet, and I fell. As I was rolling down the mountain, one robber hit me with a big rock. Then they ran away.

Gau is a charm box or protection box.

I was losing a lot of blood and was hurt very badly. My friend took me to a nearby family where I could rest. The wound was very deep on my left side. I was unable to pull the bullet out for several months, so I had a lot of pain from it. I found out later that there were actually sixty robbers in that gang and that the whole area was troubled by it. When we left this family, we heard some noise and thought it was the robbers. Soon we heard the shooting of pistols and just managed to hide behind a large rock. After awhile, five other travelers arrived, so we all proceeded together. Some of the travelers had guns and were ready to shoot. We did not see any more robbers and were able to escape from that area.

Traders camping
Photo courtesy of
The Library of Tibetan
Works and Archives,
Dharamsala, India

After some time, I went to visit a great meditator named Chatrel Sangay Dorje in Phari to consult him as to whether I should go on a pilgrimage to India. He said that it was not a very good idea at that time because I should keep doing the retreat that I had started at Dudro Monastery. I stayed three years. I then went to see him again and told him I had been having many inauspicious dreams. My mind was not very peaceful, and I felt that something was going to happen. He told me that the Chinese had already come to that area and that if I did leave Tibet, it should be to go to Nepal, not India. Some people in the area had heard that I was thinking about leaving and sent a group of people to request that I stay. I agreed that I would.

While the head of the monastery, Lama Suntrul Pema Woesel, was away, twenty–five Chinese military men, including two officers and one translator, came and questioned me. They said that they had heard I was the abbot of this monastery. They wanted to know how I managed it and how many sheep and goats it owned. They wanted a complete list of everything. I told them that I was a yogi visiting there and that the head of the monastery was away. I said I did not know exactly how much money they had, what possessions, or how many sheep because I was not working in the monastery all the time. I was just there temporarily.

The Chinese asked me if I wanted any help or money and said that if I wanted help to raise some money to support myself, they would be happy to help. I again repeated that I was not the abbot and stated that the Rinpoche who was the abbot had been incarnated seven times. All these incarnations had been in this monastery and there had not been any problem that I knew of. I told them that I thought their offer was generous, but it would be better if they asked the Tibetan government and the Dalai Lama. Following this policy was necessary since the monastery could not receive help without permission.

When the Chinese left, they gave us fifty Chinese silver coins and a package of biscuits. They offered one scarf to me and I offered one scarf to them and one to the translator. I again repeated that their help could not be accepted until they spoke to His Holiness. After one week, the Chinese came again—this time with more officers, fifty people in all. They all had guns. They asked if I had written a letter to His Holiness. When I said I had not because I was not the head lama and did not have authority to write, they asked me for the list of what was kept in the monastery—all the statues, new and old, how much money there was, among other things. I again told then that I did not have this list but I would give them a list of my things. They said that would be acceptable.

I wrote a list of what I possessed: *khatam,* a three-pronged metal staff; one goat skin; a bamboo rucksack that was full of prayer texts; a *kangling,* a bone horn; a *damaru, chod* drum; and a *Trengwa,* prayer beads. They did not like my answer. They said I was not giving a proper answer. I repeated that I did not know how many possessions the monastery owned. They told me that definitely the next time I must give them a list. I was told that I would be required to go to a special meeting with the list, or I would be punished severely.

That night after they left I did not feel very well. I had a strong pain and could not do my prayers well. An apparition appeared to me. He seemed something like a monk, but not exactly like a monk, dressed with red cloth. It was sort of an illusion. He was standing near the door, trying to frighten me. He had a sling with him and was trying to hit me with it. I did some prayers and mantras, and I threw some barley grains in his face. Then the man disappeared. But I continued to feel sick and after three days did a special ritual attributed to the Dharmapalas to recover my health. I started scolding the local protectors by calling them dogs who, instead of biting the enemy—the Chinese—spent time biting their own chain. I took off my *zhen* and started hitting the images of the local protectors. The abbot was horrified, but that night I had a sound sleep.

Zhen is a loose-fitting upper garment.

45

Ngagpa is a tantric practitioner of esoteric teachings who serves the role for the population in Tibetan culture, similar to that of a shaman or magician.

After a week, the Lama Sungtrul Pema Woesel consulted the oracle before a huge gathering. The oracle went into a trance and complained that he was not well. He was in pain, itching and having burning sensations during the trance. All the people started making offerings to him and, while making confessions for any wrongdoing, requested his forgiveness. But the oracle approached me and offered a scarf and said, "I am sorry. I never realized you were such a highly realized *Ngagpa*. When you hit me the other day and hit my wisdom mirror with your thunderbolt, it nearly broke my heart into pieces."

The abbot was very angry that I had accepted the scarf from the Chinese because they were Communists and did not believe in *dharma*. I told the abbot that I regretted my action deeply and I confessed in front of him. He then offered to protect me. I had thought my illness was because I had made a mistake in taking the money from the Chinese and that was why the apparition had appeared. After the ritual, I felt a little better. After that, the abbot and the people gained a lot of respect for me and offered me many things.

The Chinese influence in that area was very strong. They paid people to observe me and report back what I was doing and where I was going. They were also doing this with other lamas and important people. I wanted to leave to go to the other side of the country. In my area, there were herdsmen with many yaks. I spoke with the herdsmen and told them what was happening. They said not to worry, that they would tell everyone that I was going to their place to do a ritual. That way, I could get out of the area. Many lamas did not leave even though other high lamas had already been caught by the Chinese. Many were tortured, and some even killed. I left to go to the other side of the hill and do a ritual for the herdsmen. I carried only my texts and religious implements with me. From there I escaped by mule.

I did not have many problems leaving Tibet. I had some money and many Tibetan people were escaping at that time, even though many lamas were being caught. I was very fortunate. It was 1957. I went on pilgrimage through Sikkim to Nepal and India, to all the holy places and shrines of Buddhism. Then I visited Delhi and the Punjab. After the pilgrimage I returned to Darjeeling and Sikkim.

While in Gangtok, Sikkim, I dreamed of a *khadroma* who told me to go to a holy mountain, and she pointed to a mountain with a huge lake in front of it. There was a monastery near where I was staying and the next day I asked people if they knew of such a place. They directed me to Mount Kailash and Lake Manasarovar in Western Tibet.

I wanted to go there. I did not have enough money, but since I always received my messages from *khadromas*, I had to listen. And so I sold everything that I could, including some turquoise and coral which were decorating some of my religious articles and also a very expensive garment. It was a very difficult and long journey. Also, by late 1958, Tibet was already occupied by the Chinese. They did not notice me because I was wearing simple clothes and looked very poor, like a beggar. Soon after my arrival at the holy Mount Kailash, I confined myself to a monastery where I stayed in retreat for two months.

Chapter Six:

LIFE IN INDIA

In 1959, I returned to India by way of Bhutan and settled in Darjeeling. When I arrived, I did not have any money and also had no passport. When I left Sikkim for Tibet, my passport had been taken from me. I borrowed money, got a new passport, and gradually met families that wanted me to do rituals to stop the rain.

During that time I married and had two sons, Karma Sonam in 1962 and Karma Norbu in 1966. (I had previously been married and had a son in 1951 named Karma Yeshe. I was twenty–five years old and my wife and I were separated as a result of the Chinese invasion. I had been doing a pilgrimage quite far away from them at the time the Chinese came, and we were not able to escape together.) I stayed in Darjeeling nine years making and stopping the rain and hail.

Since I was known as a weather controller and the Darjeeling area was known for hailstorms and rain, I was asked by some people to stop the hailstorms. I agreed to do it for three years. I was so successful that I was asked to continue for another three years, which was followed by yet another three-year term. I really had not wanted to stay for nine years; however, I agreed to do so. At times the hail was so huge it weighed a quarter kilo (about ten ounces). This place was also famous for horse racing. Sometimes the hail was so powerful that it would kill a horse during a race.

After I had been stopping hailstorms for about seven years, I was quite well known. For this reason, the Bhotias—the local people of Darjeeling—were uneasy that a Tibetan lama was doing what they should have been doing. They simply hated the idea that someone was making and stopping the hail for them. They wanted to show that they could also do it. There were others who also claimed that they could do this for themselves without help from this foreign lama.

There was a local non-Buddhist priest performing rites to make hailstorms. I remember one time he was doing a bizzare ritual. The priest was half naked, sitting on the ground. His wife was also almost naked. On one side of her head her hair was braided; on the other, her hair hung loose. Their faces were painted red on one side and black on the other.

The woman approached her husband, carrying a rooster and a knife in her hands. While she moved around him, the priest continued performing rituals, writhing on the ground and motioning.

The priest had a fire burning in front of him. After shouting and hooting for a while, she cut the rooster and killed it. She then drank some blood and offered some to the priest. This is how they performed the hail rites. Everybody thought that there would be a harsh hailstorm for certain. It was a big success, and for more than a week there was a terrible hailstorm. I think that this is one of the reasons my health became weakened during that period. Everthing was wet and I was living very poorly. I believe that some of the ailments which I now have were aggravated because of the terrible climate at that time.

Around this time, I became quite fed up. One day, in a sudden fury, I decided to do something. I lifted up my *shabten* cup and, evoking the dieties, called out the name of this priest and said, "You want this: you have it!" I visualized throwing the cup to the priest. Sadly, there was a thunder and hailstorm a few moments later. Heavy hail fell near the house of the priest. His wife lay unconscious, in shock for several hours, due to the surprise of the storm. There was loud thunder and lightning, as if pieces of meteorites were landing. The priest's house was flooded, carrying out his belongings, while nothing happened to the other houses.

In the late 1960s, I moved to Dharamsala because I wanted to enroll my two boys in the Tibetan Children's Village, a comprehensive school that included early childhood through adult education. (My wife and I had divorced.) I lived with my sons, Kharma Sonam and Karma Norbu, in a small house in Dharamsala.

There was a big official meeting to be held in Dharamsala during the rainy season. One of the cabinet ministers of the Tibetan government–in–exile heard that I was a rainmaker and weather controller. He came and asked me if I would stop the rain during this meeting. I agreed and was commisioned by the high authorities in the government to stop the rain for the meeting, which lasted for more than ten days. It did not rain, which pleased everyone. During that time there were also performances at the Drama School where I was also asked to control the weather.

When the meeting was finished, the organizers had a personal audience with His Holiness to receive his blessing. I was also invited. His Holiness told us that he was very happy with the success of the meeting. He pointed to me and said that he was especially pleased that the rain had been stopped and that he appreciated my work.

While in Dharamsala, I remarried. Approximately two years later, my wife became ill, and I lost sight, temporarily, in one eye. My ear was also infected. Through the help of the Dalai Lama's sister, I was admitted to the Children's

Yeshe Dorje Rinpoche
Photo by Dr. Marsha Woolf

Village Hospital. Although they were very kind, they could not do anything to help my eye or ear. They sent us to a hospital in the Punjab where I had cataract surgery. My wife also received care, and we stayed for about two weeks. When we returned to Dharamsala, we moved into the Tibetan Children's Village. In 1973, we celebrated the birth of our daughter, Mingyur Chodon.

In 1974, I was invited to Manali to stop the rain that was ruining the apples, the main produce of the area. I had heard that Manali had special hot springs with healing properties, and I thought I could go there to treat my knees, which had been bothering me for some time. When I arrived I heard His Holiness was also there. I spent many hours doing rituals to stop the rain at this beautiful resort with many orchards.

When His Holiness the Dalai Lama saw me standing in a garden, he sent someone to call me. His Holiness asked me what I was doing there, and I told him that someone had requested I come and stop the rain and hail in order to save the fruit from being ruined, and that I had come also because I wanted to use the springs' healing waters. The Dalai Lama knew the man who had asked me to come. As His Holiness spoke with me, I was so nervous that I could not even remember the name of the apples. This was the first time I had spoken with His Holiness privately.

He asked me all about my religious practices and all the initiations and transmissions I had received. His Holiness asked me also what I was doing in Dharamsala and where I was staying. I told him I was doing a lot of rituals, especially on two important days every month. He was very pleased. I also told him I was living at the Children's Village with a small group of lamas trying to start a monastery.

His Holiness told me to work very hard and, if I did, I would be successful. His words sent my head into a spin, thinking about what I could achieve with poor eyesight, poor hearing, and no money. Nevertheless, he gave me a tremendous inner will to try my best, for His Holiness would not say anything that would not materialize. His Holiness also promised to visit me at Dharamsala. When I later told my disciples and associates about what he had said, they were in disbelief.

While I was at the Children's Village, there were four occasions on which I was asked to pacify spirits, or ghosts, haunting the village. The first was an angry official who turned immediately into a ghost when he died. Many people saw the ghost of this man, and everyone was frightened, especially the young children who stayed inside the house where the ghost appeared the most. Many rituals had been conducted, but they had not helped much. Then I went with a few friends and, after completing a special ritual, the ghost finally calmed down and disappeared. Around that same time there was a lady, whom people had known quite well, who also turned into a ghost after she died. People always saw her near the bus station. I also did a ritual for her and subdued her.

Another time there was a ghost at the Children's Village. The man had been a foster father to many of the children. When he died, many people saw him walking on the road leading to the Children's Village or riding a bicycle through the town. People did a lot of rituals that did not help. I was called and asked to do a special fire ritual. I went on a small retreat and followed it with the fire ritual. Finally, then, the ghost was at peace. Shortly afterwards, one girl at the Drama School died and turned into a ghost who made a lot of trouble, especially in the house during the night. I went and did rituals to pacify her.

On October 23, 1975, His Holiness made a visit to the Children's Village for an annual celebration that was held there. I knew that he was coming, so I made all the necessary preparations to receive him appropriately in my small monastery in case he should visit. (I had actually started this monastery with three lamas, and we had fifteen people who attended *shabten* regularly on the tenth and twenty–fifth days of every month. It was a small center made of burlap bags.)

On that very morning, my wife gave birth to my youngest son, Venerable Tenzin Sangpo. The other lamas did not believe that His Holiness would visit our monastery, so they went to the festivities.

After the function at the Children's Village, His Holiness started walking down the hill so briskly that even his bodyguards could not keep up. They did not even know where he was going until they got to my makeshift temple. All were surprised that His Holiness would visit such a place!

During his visit, he asked me which rituals I did in the monastery and what my plan for the future was. I told him I did not have any special plan. I had thought about moving to one of the Tibetan settlement camps in the south of India but had cancelled the idea because I was not feeling well. Problems with my eyes and ears would prevent me from working in the fields. I also told him I was concerned that this small center I had founded might not last if I left and that I wanted it to continue. His Holiness told me to be patient and he would see what could be done. At this time, the monastery was in very poor condition and in need of wood and tin. It was not a properly constructed building.

After a few days I was called to the Council for Religious and Cultural Affairs. I was asked to stay in Dharamsala and make it my residence. I was also

Kalachakra means wheel of time.

given permission to raise some funds and to accept donations of books to help the monastery.

Shortly after the visit of His Holiness to the Children's Village, he planned a trip to Ladakh to give the *kalachakra* initiation. The head lama of the monastery there wrote to invite me to come and stop the rain. The office of His Holiness also requested me to go on this trip. We went from the monastery in Dharamsala to Kashmir on a bus provided by His Holiness, and then by ten jeeps to Ladakh. I stayed in a tent near the initiation place and stopped the rain.

The next day His Holiness asked me if I had been told to stop the rain totally, to which I replied, "Yes." His Holiness explained that I should allow the rain to fall the next day since it is considered auspicious to have a "welcome rain" during the teachings. I told His Holiness I would definitely try my best to have the rain fall. I started the necessary rituals immediately, and the next day there was the heaviest rain and snow that had ever fallen at that time of year. The snow was so heavy that many people had problems coming to attend the teachings.

The next day the secretary to His Holiness asked me to stop the rain and snow before His Holiness granted initiation. So I performed the ritual from dawn to dusk in order to stop the heavy rain and control the weather. I had been blowing my horn so much that I had cuts on my mouth. During the actual initiation the sky was overcast, and it drizzled in all places except on the huge ground where people were standing to receive the initiation. The sun shone on the teaching ground. Everyone was amazed by this miracle.

On the final day of the teachings, the organizers gathered to receive a special blessing from His Holiness. Many people also approached me for a special blessing, which made me feel very uneasy. I believe that all of this making and stopping the rain was successful because of the blessing of His Holiness the Dalai Lama himself.

While we were living at the Children's Village, my youngest son was recognized as a Rinpoche who is a *tulku*, a reincarnated being of a very great Tibetan lama. After he was recognized, at a very young age, we sent him to a Nyingmapa monastery in the Tibetan settlement at Bylakuppe in South India. When he is old enough, he will return to his main monastery in Nepal, where he served in his previous life.

The main reason I was asked to stay in Dharamsala was to stop the rain on special occasions. When the Children's Village needed the place where I was staying to build a hostel, I had to move. The office of His Holiness contacted me to ask if I had any permanent residential

Venerable Tenzin Sangpo, son of Yeshe Dorje Rinpoche
Photo courtesy of Zilnon Kagyeling Monastery

Venerable Sonan Tenzin, Tenzin Sangpo's previous incarnation
Photo courtesy of Zilnon Kagyeling Monastery

place, which I did not. They offered me a plot of land below the Tibetan Institute of Performing Arts and agreed to sponsor me because His Holiness wanted to establish a Nyingmapa monastery in Dharamsala. Then he would have each of the four sects of Tibetan Buddhism in Dharamsala. My responsibility was to build the monastery.

The reason His Holiness selected me to start this monastery is that I had a direct lineage to this tradition. Before starting construction, I went to visit my teacher His Holiness Dudjom Rinpoche in Nepal for four months. Aside from going to receive his teachings, I also went to ask him for his expertise to gather all the ancient Nyingma texts from the Nyingmapa lineage for my monastery in Dharamsala. Construction of the monastery began in 1979, and I made periodic journeys to South India to raise funds from the Tibetan people.

Today, one of the main aims of the monastery is to serve as a retreat center for those monks, as well as lay people, who want to practice the three-year, three-month, three-day retreat. Eleven rooms were constructed, and there are eighteen students in all: eight monks who can undertake the long retreat and ten other students who study Buddhist philosophy and other monastic teachings. There is one monk to manage the retreats, one teacher to guide the students, and a chief administrator to oversee everything.

Chapter Seven:
BUILDING THE MONASTERY

During the talks about planning my monastery with His Holiness the Dalai Lama and His Holiness Dudjom Rinpoche, they told me they wanted a Nyingma monastery and retreat place that would focus on Kagyed teachings practiced by the Fifth Dalai Lama. Kagyed teachings are commonly associated with Nyingma teachings. However, for a true *dharma* practitioner, the relevance of the concepts of Kagyed can be found in all four schools: Sakya, Gelug, Kagyu, and Nyingma. The concept of Kagyed includes all the major sects of Tibetan Buddhism, and they are represented by different deities.

There are many deities divided into eight sections of teachings. The principal deity, which is present in the entire eight sections, is Chechok. This deity is found in an erotic pose with the female component, better known as the Yab–Yum pose or the father–mother pose. The mother or Yum aspect has nine heads and eighteen hands. The father aspect, Yab, has twenty–one heads and forty–two hands. All of the hands are holding different implements. Generally speaking, the Yab is the peaceful form in meditation. His features, implements, and *mudras* are all peaceful. Although Yab and Yum have aspects of both peace and wrath, Yum, the mother, is generally represented as the wrathful aspect. Her *mudras*, gestures, and the implements she holds all represent the wrathful aspect of Chechok.

The concept of Kagyed was present in Tibet long before Buddhism fragmented into the four sects. It was the first form of Buddhism. Therefore, the Kagyed is the springboard or the main source of different lineages of different sages and lamas in Tibet. Chechok is depicted suppressing eight deities, eight nags—deities from the underworld—beneath their feet. The word *ka*, from which Kagyed comes, is the root word which means sphere of *dharma*. The *ka* is not exclusive to any form of teaching or sect. The *dharma* sphere embodies the vast expanse of knowledge. *Kagyed* literally means eight orders, or testaments, granted by Padmasambhava to eight special disciples of his time. Each of these eight testaments has a special deity. All of the eight combined into one is represented by Chechok.

The present name of the monastery is Zilnon Kagyed Ling. The name was

Mudra is a sanskrit word for sacred gesture symbolizing inner wisdom.

given by His Holiness the Dalai Lama. *Zilnon* means the subduer. The monastery is dedicated to His Holiness Dudjom Rinpoche.

The first statue made for the monastery is one of Guru Nangsid Zilnon, a wrathful form of Padmasambhava. It is said that the sight of him is enough to subdue all beings. In 1987, I had been preparing the monastery to accommodate a three–year, three–month, and three–day retreat for eight monks. I requested that His Holiness the Dalai Lama inaugurate this monastery as well as the commencement of the retreat. On October 1, 1987, there was the first peaceful demonstration in Tibet. At the same time it was going on, I was leading a wrathful ceremony at the monastery. In other words, while tensions were escalating in Tibet, we were saying special prayers in the monastery.

On October 4, a few days later, His Holiness came to inaugurate my monastery. It was the first grand official function at my monastery. My monastery was flooded with thousands of people. Over five hundred people, including all of the heads of the monasteries and officials, both Tibetan and Indian, were invited to a ceremony to mark the opening of the monastery as well as the three–year retreat. It was my pleasure to host a lunch for all those formally invited at the hall of T.I.P.A. It was a whole–day affair. His Holiness presided over all of the functions and ceremonies. He was very

His Holiness the Dalai Lama wearing the Guru Rinpoche hat, October 4, 1987
Photo courtesy of Zilnon Kagyeling Monastery

pleased at the work that had been completed. There was so much to do that day that the actual formal empowerment or invitation was set forth at a later date. Meanwhile, His Holiness left for Manali.

Soon after his return from Manali, His Holinesss conferred the full Dagnang Sangwa Gyachen initiation to the retreatants and a huge gathering at the main temple on November 14 and 15. It was another rare event of celebration under the sponsorship of Zilnon Kagyed Ling Monastery. Although I originally had intended to have eight monks, six were blessed by His Holiness before entering the retreat. I am determined to have eight in the next one.

Since then I have been working very hard, going to many places to raise funds to support these monks while they are in retreat. After they finish this retreat, they will have to change quarters within the monastery and make way for eight more monks who will then begin their three–year, three–month, three–day retreat. They must have their own meditation and living space, which I must build soon.

Actually, these retreats can be organized on a grand scale as well. In this case, from the very beginning, it was a small venture. Space is a problem, as well as finding the right type of person to go into a retreat. In the future, if I get the land, I can expand the monastery to accommodate more people in retreat.

Shedra is a spiritual school.

My original idea was to have a *shedra* attached to the monastery. When I am able to start the school, there are certain Nyingmapa lamas who will send their students to the school. It will be a center for learning and the presentation of Nyingmapa. There is a problem with lack of land upon which to build this school. The present land the monastery is on formerly belonged to T.I.P.A. and was given to us by His Holiness the Dalai Lama. The adjacent land belongs to the Indian Forest Department, and I am not certain if it can be made available for this purpose. I am hopeful that good things will happen for this monastery in my lifetime. I have a small supplication prayer given by His Holiness Dudjom Rinpoche for my monastery. I am sure the power of this supplication will enable me to accomplish what I envision.

What encouraged me in the first place was that during an audience with His Holiness Dudjom Rinpoche, he patted me on the back, saying that I do have the potential and inclination to take on the work of preserving and promoting the Kagyed tradition. He said, "You are destined to do this by your karmic force. You are bound to succeed." That gave me enormous encouragement, and I started going here and there, approaching people like you, Marsha, and here we are! I would never have dreamed that I would be able to do these things. I have worked very hard to develop the monastery. I hope someday the local authorities will allow me to use the adjoining land or give it on lease.

I have an excellent associate, Venerable Khamtul Rinpoche, given to me by His Holiness to help with the teaching. He is a highly realized tantric practitioner who was former secretary of the Council for Cultural and Religious Affairs. He visits the monastery periodically to help with instruction.

One of the main practices at my monastery dates back to the time of the Fifth Dalai Lama. I am the first incarnation of Migyur Dorje. He was a lama who was a highly realized being at that time.

Story as told to Dr. Marsha Woolf

Purba is also the name of a special ritual sceptre.

Terton is a treasure finder.

He established the Dongag Choeling Monastery, and his main practice was the same as that of the Fifth Dalai Lama. Dagnang Sangwa Gyachen is a special teaching that was followed voluntarily by the great Fifth Dalai Lama by going to the famous Nyingma monastery, Mindroling. He not only practiced the teachings but also had visions of the deity *Purba*, belonging to this special form of teaching. The Fifth Dalai Lama had many great teachings through his visions of the deity Purba. Many texts of this tradition including those written by His Holiness the Fifth Dalai Lama are now preserved in the Library of Tibetan Works and Archives in Dharamsala. The Fifth Dalai Lama is considered one of 108 *Terton* teachers in Tibetan history.

This lineage from the Fifth Dalai Lama has come down through the years unbroken, although it has not been used by many. The great texts from that time were not compiled daily or edited properly and so they just sat in various places vitually untouched. All of the Dalai Lamas continued to follow this practice. The present Dalai Lama calls this teaching the father religion, or *Phachos*, tracing the source of one's spiritual father. So the present Dalai Lama has taken a great interest in reviving this tradition. When this task was handed over to me, I had to depend upon His Holiness Dudjom Rinpoche for the finer details of these teachings since he and His Holiness the Dalai Lama were the two primary lamas who had information. Some of the texts were missing, left or lost in Tibet. In 1985, the great tantric teacher Dilgo Khentse Rinpoche found some of these texts unused on reserve shelves in American libraries. He sent them to His Holiness the Dalai Lama, which proved very helpful to me.

Now a start has been made. It is my responsibility to have these retreats continue, uninterrupted. The ultimate goal is not only to run these long retreats, but to see that all aspects of Nyingma and Kagyed teachings are covered. We also have to see that all the monks coming out of meditation after the long retreat have proper, permanent accommodations so that they can begin their real work, living a religious life.

Even if we regain our country and return to establish a main monastery in Tibet, this will still remain a center for retreats in India. The idea is to really keep it running even after my death. It will be the responsibility of the others, including my son, who is presently being trained in a monastery in southern India, to see that it continues. As far as the idea for a school goes, it will start on a small scale, maybe ten to fifteen students, and will increase gradually.

Although we have diffferent nomenclatures—Sakyapas, Gelugpas, Kagyudpas, and Nyingmapas—in terms of philosophical debates for intellectual exercises and for academic development, in the final analysis of the realization of one's practice, everyone strives for *Dzog Chen,* the Great Completion. Just as we have these different sects which can be compared to a lovely mandala which has four gates that ultimately lead to the same main deity in the center, the same is true for all forms of Buddhism. The ultimate source or ultimate refuge or the ultimate teacher has to be Buddha himself and the religion, Buddhism. We have these different names and practices only for the purpose of making teachings suitable for different people. We all have different dispositions, capabilities, and aptitudes. For some, tantra or Nyingma is the right teaching. For others, the ideal path is Gelug. So that is really how the different sects came to be, to suit the individual, but in the final analysis, it is Buddha and Buddhism.

It is like a doctor. The word doctor is a general term. One doctor cannot help everybody, all diseases. Many doctors specialize, for example, on the skin, the eyes, or teeth. The main idea is to help the patient, to find the right doctor. So *Dharma* or *Choe* is there. The idea of a religious man is to be compassionate, show love and kindness, have nothing to hide, and be able to help others in whatever way he can. If not, then one is not to harm or bring suffering or add to others' sufferings. In other words, help;

if not, do not harm. That is the idea. One who brings harm or creates more problems cannot be a religious man.

Even in Tibetan Buddhism we have different schools. Each is for a special purpose, and yet you find people saying Nyingmapa is bad, Kagyudpa is good, or Gelugpa is this or that. It simply shows that this person does not understand the whole idea behind the schools. It is like saying there is no hell because I have not seen it. So religion is the science of the mind: the idea is to train and control the mind. There cannot be two different kinds of minds and sentient beings. They are the same thing. There are different ways of managing the mind. The idea is to train and cleanse the mind and strive to make the mind perfect.

So, Marsha, we can simply compare a doctor and a religious man. A religious man tries to heal everyone's mind from illusions and delusions, just as a doctor tries to heal the patient of a disease. Therefore, the religious man and the doctor are the best ones to understand why one should generate love, compassion, and service to others. Everyone can have this kind of attitude, but it is very special with religious teachers and doctors. It is an integral part of their practice.

I am very hopeful that when this book comes out that it is a nice piece of work showing people that when one maintains one's courage and determination, it is possible to achieve, against seemingly insurmountable obstacles, very high results. This is the simple truth of my story and of my life. I would like it to be a source of inspiration for all those to see that here is someone who has worked hard.

Yeshe Dorje Rinpoche
December 16, 1990
Photo by David Johnston

EPILOGUE

For the last thirty-four years, stories continue of severe human rights violations in Tibet. A fact-finding delegation sent by His Holiness the Dalai Lama was allowed into Tibet in 1979. They heard first-hand accounts of mandatory abortions on Tibetan women, sterilization of Tibetan men, and mass extermination of their people. Millions of Chinese Hans—pure Chinese—had been relocated into Tibet. The Tibetans at that point were outnumbered three to one, or more than half of their native land.

The current situation in Tibet heightened in March, 1989, with the violence and imposition of martial law by the Chinese Communists. More than 170,000 troops were stationed in Lhasa while thousands of Tibetans now living in India and elsewhere staged peaceful marches in support of their countrymen. Many people were tortured, killed, or imprisoned during this period. All foreign tourists and correspondents had to leave. In June, 1993, another uprising resulted in the same repressive behavior by the Chinese government.

As more and more Tibetan refugees escape to India, additional reports of atrocities continue to be heard. A former political prisoner of twenty-two years states,

"Chinese treatment of Tibetan prisoners is beyond human understanding. Sanitation, nutritional diet, medical attention, and clothing were non–existent. Human flesh, horse and dog meat were part of our diets. Ninety percent of the prison population lost their lives because of execution and starvation."

Still the Tibetans remain dedicated to their belief that their country will be free some day and that His Holiness the Dalai Lama will return to his palace, the *Potala,* now being used as a tourist attraction by the Chinese. For many years, His Holiness the Dalai Lama has traveled extensively throughout the world, asking the international community to appeal to China on behalf of his people and to educate the world about the human rights abuses in his homeland. He received the 1989 Nobel Peace Prize for his continued efforts to seek a nonviolent solution to the conflict between Tibet and China, and he continues to instill hope in his people.

Today, with part of Yeshe Dorje Rinpoche's monastery completed, contruction goes on. Until his recent death, he journeyed within India, making and stopping the rain and performing *shabtens*. He also visited different countries and established a base in the United States in an attempt to bring a greater understanding of Tibetan Buddhism to the West.

INTERVIEW ON MEDITATION WITH YESHE DORJE RINPOCHE

by Dr. Marsha Woolf

MW: One has heard a lot of the word meditation. What does it mean?

YD: Meditation is the name for the technique of the practice of religion or *dharma*. Anything that one practices is meditation. If one does not practice on a daily basis, it cannot be meditation.

We come to meditation, wanting to do something solid, having a desire to free ourselves and others in the face of this world. One should be able to visualize with great compassion and love all sentient beings, including ourselves.

When we speak of meditation, the practice has to be with the knowledge that we will die someday. One must also acknowledge the fact that nothing in the material world is going to help us—not money, fame, where we live, will help. So meditation cannot be on this aspect of existence. Meditation, when practiced properly, is a part of daily life.

MW: What is *dharma*?

YD: The term *dharma* or *choe*, the Tibetan name for religion, is not an exclusive term. It embodies all the religions of the world, including, Buddhism, Christianity, Hinduism, Judaism. When we accept that there are religions, we also accept the broad principles of these religions—their spiritual and moral laws. From that perspective we can have compassion and sympathy for someone in distress or difficulty. A fundamental aspect of religion is to have this compassion for those who are suffering.

To show concern, sympathy, or compassion for someone who is suffering is a starting point. Then we can go one step further. If there is someone lying on the road, disabled and shabby, you can go beyond simply feeling concern for this man, and think about what you can do for him. Although your help may be very minor, a simple word to give him solace or a hand to help him to move to a place more comfortable without any thought of "Oh, he's a dirty man, why should I touch him?" is an act of compassion. If you can accept the fact that here is someone like me who is in distress and I must help him no matter in how small a way, then this is also the practice of religion.

Another example would be if someone were lying on the road thirsty and unable to move. All this person needs is some water. Anyone is able to help him with a cup of water. Although it is a very small amount of help that one is giving and a very common act, many people will do it without thinking. If you think about it properly, you are performing a religious act. You could be saving a life by giving him a cup of water, although it is a small sacrifice for you. Even if one does not know the finer details of religious philosophies, the meditations, the rituals, one can have this compassion.

MW: How can one learn to concentrate?

YD: The idea is to have control of the mind. Imagine the mind as if it were a horse. The body rides the horse, and the mind can take you everywhere. It is the mind that leads you, initiates you, to do what you do.

Although all orders come from the mind, the mental spectrum, an example of the fickleness of the mind can be explained in terms of wealth. The fickle mind can go crazy with happiness when you have a bonus or windfall of wealth. If it is not properly used, just possessing wealth is not good enough to bring you happiness. It can be the cause of your downfall and of your suffering if you misuse it. The wealth, the sorrow, the sad period we are facing, are all passing times. They come and go.

MW: How often should one meditate?

YD: One should try to meditate, if possible, four times a day—the morning, afternoon, evening and nighttime. If you are too busy, one should do it twice—in the morning and before one goes to sleep. This is very important.

MW: If one is very busy, what is the minimum time one should give to meditation?

YD: The timing can vary from person to person. It also depends on the kind of meditation one is doing. The important thing is to meditate using as much concentration as you can. Even if you have time, if you're not able to focus, there's no point. So a short time with good concentration could be enough.

MW: How long must one meditate before one can expect to see a change in oneself?

YD: It depends upon the person's intellectual capacity and the ability to concentrate. For instance, someone practicing the transference of consciousness, what we call the *powa* practice, might notice changes within three days. With others it could take much longer.

MW: Rinpoche, what is *chod*?

YD: *Chod* is that doctrine which is the basis for the deliverance of human beings from this world to achieve Buddhahood, or nirvana. We are all born and will die someday. That is a fact. In order to achieve Buddhahood, we have to rely on the three objects of refuge—Buddha, *dharma*, and *sangha*. Deliverance from this world is through the

<u>Sangha</u> is a Buddhist community of monks and nuns, lay initiates, and practitioners.

means of achieving nirvana or the total deliverance from this cyclic world of existence, for which it is important to practice the Nyingma Tradition.

MW: We hear about the different sects of Tibetan Buddhism, of the *sutras* and of *tantra*. What is so special about *tantra* in the Nyingma tradition?

YD: We can compare Nyingma tradition, like other schools of Tibetan Buddhism, to different roads all leading to the same place. *Sutrayana* can be compared to the slow and steady highway—the long way, the easy way, the time-consuming way. This method emphasizes gradual development to reach one's goal. The special thing about the *tantrayana* or the Nyingma teachings is that it is like a snake trapped in bamboo: there are only two ways to get out, one end or the other.

Tantra is that tradition, which if practiced properly, can definitely elevate you to nirvana very quickly. It is like taking shortcuts to reach your goal. Often the shortcuts are the most dangerous roads, and if you take them, you are sure to reach your goal before anybody else. However, if you are not fit or prepared and you make an ill attempt, you could end up losing your life or having a terrible experience. When *tantra* is practiced properly, miracles can happen, and it is possible to obtain enlightenment even in one's lifetime. It is said that if one is really able to concentrate on

Santras refers to the sacred texts of Buddhism.

Tantra refers to teachings of particular techniques and rituals, especially dealing with meditative practices.

Yeshe Dorje Rinpoche performing a Mo, a special Tibetan form of spiritual divination
Photo by Philip Hemley

tantra, because of its nature, one can achieve a very high level of spiritual advancement in a short time. However, it is a road only for those who are fit. The significance of *tantra* in today's jet–set age, as prophesied by Padmasambhava, is very relevant. We often hear great people, including His Holiness the Dalai Lama, state the need to worship and practice the Nyingma teachings.

MW: How does one seek spiritual guidance?

YD: Through the power of your body, speech, and mind. With your body you should make prostrations and offerings, go on pilgrimages, and engage in religious activities. Your speech should be busy collecting and reciting texts and mantras. The third, your mind, should also have pure inclination and motivation throughout your life to think in terms of the welfare of all sentient beings, always aspiring to get freedom from this cycle of the suffering world. In other words, one should try to cleanse oneself in body, speech, and mind. Always try to maintain contact with spiritual people and communities. Invite people to your house for prayers and teachings. One should always be conscious of suffering and one's desire to free oneself and all other sentient beings from this cycle of existence. It is important to have a spiritual teacher who can guide you in your prayers or teachings. He is the one who can guide you about the things to do and the things not to do, in other words, how to collect merit and to avoid collecting non–virtuous acts.

MW: How does one go about finding a spiritual teacher, a guru or lama, which you have said is very important?

YD: It is very important that we develop or cultivate the worship in a lama. It is said that even lamas should take refuge in a lama. Even incarnated beings will take refuge in a lama initially, and then take refuge in the lama in the form of the *dharma* religion. And then, finally, one would take refuge in oneself, considering oneself manifesting as an object of worship. The lama will guide us on our spiritual path, and if we are able, then we can take refuge in perfecting ourselves through these studies, texts, and prayers. If one is able to achieve this second stage, then one is in a position to look into one's mind and consciousness.

MW: Do you have a message for the people in the West?

YD: Constantly keep watch on your activities. Try to improve yourself as much as possible by staying away from negative action or poisonous feelings like pride, jealousy, or ignorance. Improve yourself by engaging in virtuous acts and try to eliminate non–virtuous ones.

APPENDIX

Commentary on Tibetan Buddhism *

By His Holiness the Dalai Lama

The many scriptures set forth in the teachings of Buddha are included in three scriptural collections. How is it that all of the Buddha's teachings are included in three scriptural collections? It is that the Buddha set forth the three trainings. The three trainings are included in the three scriptural collections, because each of them serves as the means of expressing mainly one of those collections, one of those trainings. What are the three trainings? They are the trainings in ethics—the trainings as set forth include the mode of behavior. Then there is the training in meditative stabilization, which explains how to meditate. The *Dharma* is practiced indeed by way of body, speech, and mind, but it is mainly by way of mind. One needs to tame the mind. One needs a strong mind, a concentrated mind; therefore, one needs to develop calm abiding. In the effort to attain wisdom, what we don't want is suffering, and in order to get rid of suffering, we need intelligence that can discriminate between the good and bad and so forth; therefore, we need wisdom.

The scriptures that take these three respectively as the main object of teaching

* Excerpts from *The Dalai Lama's Historic Visit to North America,* Clear Light Publications, Inc., 1981.

His Holiness the Dalai Lama with Yeshe Dorje Rinpoche
Photos courtesy of Zilnon Kagyeling Monastery

are the scriptural collection of discipline, the scriptural collection of the set of discourses, and the scriptural collection of knowledge. The training in ethics is concerned with behavior; the training in meditative stabilization is concerned with meditation; the training in wisdom is concerned with view. There is the triad; view, behavior, and meditation. The scriptures set forth a mode by which one's view, behavior, and meditation will not fall in either of the two extremes.

The scriptures on discipline set forth modes of behavior for a lay person and for monks and nuns. In the discipline, it sets forth a prohibition of the extremes of having too good clothing, food, shelter, and so forth. And the Buddha also prohibited the extreme of self–torture, in which one engages in too much fasting, or wears clothing that is not appropriate such that it brings suffering to one's self. Therefore, our proper behavior is achieved in the proper context of not falling into either of these two extremes. As Shantideva said in his *Engaging in Bodhisattva Deeds,* "The main thing is to consider the situation; what is needed in the situation."

When one puts these precepts into practice, one needs to consider that which is to be done, and the purpose. For instance, for a monk or a nun, it is not permitted to eat after 2 p.m. However, there are exceptions–for instance, if a person has an illness such that if that person didn't eat, it would increase the illness. Similarly, also one is not allowed to lie. For instance, if someone would have a vow to tell the truth, and is in the woods, and sees an animal run off in a certain direction, and then the hunter comes along and asks the person where the animal went, there is a prohibition against lying, but the purpose here would be for the sake of saving the life of that animal. Therefore, at that time, the person who even had the vow not to lie can say, "Oh, I really didn't see anything," or "I saw something in the trees." Illustrated by this, one has to take into account that which is prohibited and the probable benefit of doing something some other way, and do that which is more beneficial.

Then with respect to meditation: for instance, if one's mind comes under the influence of factors that are not consistent with meditative stabilization, such as excitement or laxity, then that is one extreme. The purpose of overcoming the distractions of laxity or excitement is to make one's mind so that one is capable of meditating on the actual mode of existence of phenomena, so that one can cultivate a true view, but if one having gotten rid of laxity and excitement, only cultivates a non–conceptual state, then that is an extreme, and that state will only lead to another lifetime of rebirth in cyclical existence, in a higher type of realm. So roughly speaking, that is a way of avoiding the two extremes, through the effects of meditation.

Then when one explains the view, this is done in terms of the two truths. Sometimes this is expressed as appearance and emptiness. All systems, whether Buddhist or non-Buddhist, present their view in terms of avoiding the two extremes of permanence and nihilism: the Santyas, the Vedantas, or within Buddhism, the Vaibhasikas, the Sautrantikas, the Chittamatrins, and the Madhyamikas.

For instance, within the Buddhist systems themselves, from within their own specific viewpoint, each of them to their own mind, has set forth a view that avoids the two extremes. However, when their views are analyzed with subtle reasoning, then the higher school finds the lower schools to have fallen into extremes of permanence or nihilism. So then, how is it that the higher schools can refute the lower, given that both are based on Buddhist teachings?

In the Buddhist system, the Buddha set forth the four reliances: Do not rely on the person; rely on the doctrine. You cannot say that a doctrine is to be valued just because a person who teaches it is something wonderful. Rather, it is the case that whether the person is reliable or not is to be proved in relation to the reliability or lack of reliability of the doctrine that the person teaches.

Then, with respect to the doctrine, one shouldn't rely on the euphony, and so forth, of the word, but look to the profundity of those words. Then, with respect to the teachings, one should not rely on the meaning to be interpreted, but on the definitive meaning. And with respect to the meaning, one should not rely on the consciousness that is deluded or affected by dualistic perception, but should rely on an exalted wisdom consciousness, free from such dualistic appearances.

Therefore, the teacher, Buddha himself, said, "Oh monks and nuns, you should not accept my teaching just out of respect for me, but should analyze it, the way that a goldsmith analyzes gold by rubbing, cutting and melting." Therefore, although Buddha himself set forth several means of distinguishing his own scriptures with respect to whether they were definitive or interpretable, it is by reasoning that we must determine which is definitive and which is interpretable.

Thus it is that the entire system, with subtler and subtler reasoning, shows that the two of the lower systems fall into the two extremes. How is it, in the Madhyamika system, that they avoid the two extremes? They avoid the extreme of permanence by viewing that phenomena do not exist in their own right. And it is through that knowledge of how to present all the actions, objects of cyclic existence and nirvana–how to present all phenomena within the context of their not inherently existing, but existing conventionally, validly—that they avoid the extreme of non–existence or nihilism.

It is truly mind that sees the actual mode of subsistence of phenomena. It is the mind that acts as an antidote to the types of aimless consciousness that misconceive the nature of phenomena. And it is through removing that ignorance that one can remove the desire and hatred and so forth that are induced by that ignorance. When one can stop that, one can stop the accumulation of contaminated action, or karma. Through stopping that, one stops birth. Through stopping birth, one stops suffering. Such a training in wisdom can only be achieved by the mind, therefore, it is necessary to make the mind serviceable. Therefore, I see it as necessary prior to the training in wisdom to engage in the training of meditative stabilization.

It is not being said that in order to generate a consciousness arisen through hearing or arisen from thinking that realizes emptiness, it is necessary at first to engage in training of meditative stabilization. What is being said is that in order to generate a consciousness which has arisen from meditation, and realizes emptiness, it is necessary at first to engage in the training of meditative stabilization.

In order to overcome the internal distractions within the mind, it is necessary at first to overcome the distractions of body and speech through proper ethics. Therefore, the training in ethics is set forth first. But the series of degrees is set forth in their series of practices. That is the explanation of how to avoid the two extremes in relation to the three trainings.

New Buddhists in Western society need also to avoid the two extremes. One of these extremes would be complete isolation from the general way of life, and also from society. That is the same thing. It is better to remain in society and to lead a general way of life. That's my belief.

And the other extreme would be to become completely absorbed in this worldly life, to become so involved in making money that one becomes a part in a machine. So you have to avoid those two extremes.

You have to practice kindness and follow the teachings. At the same time, if you always practice tolerance, compassion, sometimes some people may take advantage of you. On that occasion, without losing your internal calmness, your internal compassion, you may take action of some nature in order to prevent someone from taking advantage of you. That is a practical way. You have to avoid the extreme, too, of being taken advantage of. At all times, one needs to avoid the two extremes. If you get too hungry, the same—if you gorge yourself, the same also.

So my true religion is kindness. If you practice kindness as you live, no matter if you are learned or not learned, whether you believe in the next life or not, whether you believe in God or Buddha or some other religion, in day–to–day life, you have to be a kind person. With this motivation, whether you are a practitioner, or lawyer, politician, administrator, worker, or engineer, it does not matter. Whatever your profession or field, you carry your work as a professional. In the meantime, deep down, you are a kind person. This is something useful in our daily life.

AFTERWORD

Tibet Today *

The Dalai Lama as Moral Leader

by Professor Robert A.F. Thurman

I am pleased to tell you today about Tibet. It is as far away as any land can get on this round earth. Yet it is also very close. The Chinese overlords there have cut off communications, and more Tibetans have been arrested and taken off to prisons. Others who were locked up were surely interrogated, tortured into confessions and accusations. And more of those already condemned were surely executed.

To understand the situation in Tibet today, the first fact we need to know is that Tibet has always been a free country since the beginning of her recorded history around 300 B.C. She spawned a powerful conquest dynasty, which held a huge empire together from the sixth to the ninth century. Her written language and first written law code date from the seventh century, a hundred years before the first English writings in Roman script, two hundred before Charlemagne's law code, six hundred before Magna Carta. She began the process of conversion from militaristic imperialism to peaceful Buddhism in the fifth century. A clear case can be made that

* Address originally given at the Unitarian Church in Providence, Rhode Island, May 1, 1987.

she carried the Buddhi–cization process further than any other nation in history and therefore was, until 1950, the most "Buddhistically advanced" culture on the planet. Thus, the legal, moral, and actual independence of Tibet throughout her history is easily determined by even a casual perusal of the available reputable scholarship. The unique preciousness of Tibetan civilization takes considerably great effort to discover and articulate, though many people have somehow sensed the power of her spiritual blessings, shining from her snowy peaks out into a troubled world.

Since the Chinese Eighth Army began the invasion of Tibet in October 1950, the physical products of her culture have been utterly destroyed, first by the Red Army and then by the Red Guards. Over a million people have been caused to die. A generation has been deprived of education and knowledge of its own culture. Over 6,000 large monasteries, over 10,000 temples and hermitages, and countless religious monuments have been desecrated and demolished down to the foundations. Priceless statues and icons have been smashed and melted or stolen and sold; rare books treasured for millennia have been burned by the millions. The land has been depleted, the forests clear–cut, the wildlife destroyed, the people rendered economically destitute. The spiritual core of their Buddhist life has been violated. Finally, the present Chinese policy is to complete this genocide by assimilation through population transfer, importing millions of Chinese colonists to occupy all the best spots, while removing thousands of the last generation of Tibetan children for education and acculturation all over China. The Dalai Lama's Office of Information, which keeps meticulous, village–by–village records, through constantly updated eye–witness observations of Chinese activities in Tibet, projects that this population transfer tactic will have completed the marginalization of Tibetans in Tibet within two years, at the rate maintained since 1983.

For this reason, His Holiness the Dalai Lama is emerging from thirty years of relative political silence and beginning a new nonviolent activism, in the civil disobedience tradition of Thoreau, Gandhi, and King. He feels he must take the risk now and expose the duplicity and destructiveness of the rulers of China, from Mao to Deng, with whom he has maintained a conversation since 1954. The Tibetan people themselves, as they have recently shown, are still ready to give their lives to demonstrate the reality of their situation.

To describe Tibet, I used the phrase "Buddhistically advanced." Every Buddhist considers one's human life each individual's precious attainment. One experiences as a certainty its connection with eons of previous lives, most of a much more difficult, much more limited, animal nature. And one regards with real fear and trembling the danger of being dragged onward into future eons of such troublesome lives. Such an outlook powerfully motivates the Buddhist individual to use the human lifetime to the fullest extent possible to develop that freedom from blind instinctual drives and that mastery of wise and benevolent energies that are required to achieve the complete

Henry David Thoreau, 1817-1862, American writer, philosopher

Mohandas K. Gandhi, 1869-1948, Indian Nationalist, spiritual leader

Martin Luther King, 1929-1968, American clergyman, political leader

assurance that the inevitable death–transition can be negotiated without danger or loss.

In a society where many individuals are so motivated, it obviously becomes important that social matters are arranged in such a way that there is minimal interference with the individual's life–and–death urgent purpose and that there is optimal opportunity and assistance for that purpose. Historically most societies have not been so based on the individual's urgent quest for freedom and enlightenment—in fact the very possibility of such achievable freedom has dawned in rather few. So in those societies the individual's purpose must conform to those of the group, say producing children, collecting food and wealth, waging wars to gain dominion, serving of overlords, human and divine, and so forth. When the Buddhist vision of individual destiny and life purpose enters any such society, there is clearly a kind of quiet revolution. In ancient India, the Buddha founded an alternative society, his Jewel Society, the core of which was the monastic institution he invented. This Jewel Society slowly grew within the more group–oriented society until it began to transform it. It moved out into other societies in all directions, and helped countless individuals discover freedom, thereby transforming those societies; however, there was always tension. Ultimately, India lost its Jewel Society when its later authorities decided such individualism was no longer tolerable. In other countries, there was always a seesaw between rulers with their armies and sages with their monks.

Out of all of them, it was only in Tibet that the Jewel Society and its monastic core finally assumed control over the ordinary society—the head monk, the foremost sage, became the ruler of the land. It took a thousand years, from 640 to 1640. And it produced a unique society—one with no military at all, one where the education of individuals was the major business of government through its monastic universities, one where economic development was harnessed to maximize the individual citizen's spiritual development, one where each was primarily oriented toward individual evolutionary progress, according to ability and circumstances. Apparently, many individuals did succeed in achieving real nirvana, freedom from instinctual drives, and real enlightenment, and mastery of wise and loving energies. And so even the great number who were not so able were encouraged by their success, were delighted to live close with them, were inspired to direct themselves to gain such abilities themselves in succeeding lives. This, in brief sketch, is what I mean by a "Buddhistically advanced" nation. There is a great deal to learn from such a nation on many levels, from its arts and sciences, its culture, its government and institutions. We should not allow such a civilization to become extinct.

Robert A.F. Thurman
Professor of Religion
Columbia University

GLOSSARY

Bardo – place of transition between lifetimes; the place where one goes after death before the next incarnation

Chod – exorcism in Nyingma tradition; also means cutting attachment

Chodpas – practitioners of exorcism

Dakini – female angelic deity; also called *khadroma*

Choe – Tibetan name for religion

Dharma – common name for all religions or any love or compassion traditions

Gau – charm box, protection box

Guru – spiritual teacher

Kalachakra – wheel of time

Khadroma – female angelic deity; also called *dakini*

Lama – spiritual teacher

Lung gom – meditation technique utilizing subtle internal airs or winds of body

Mandala – Hindu or Buddhist graphic symbol of universe, specifically a circle enclosing a square with a deity on each side

Mudra – sanskit word for sacred gesture symbolizing inner wisdom

Ngagpa (Nagakpa) – tantric practitioner of esoteric teachings who serves the role for the population in Tibetan culture, similar to that of shaman or magician

Nyingma – oldest of four Tibetan Buddhist sects; others are Kagyu, Gelug, and Sakya

Powa – transference of consciousness

Purba – name of a deity; also name of special ritual sceptre

Rinpoche – "precious one," title given to incarnated and highly–realized beings

Sangha – Buddhist community of monks and nuns, lay initiates, and practitioners

Shabten – rituals, prayer ceremonies; also called *pooja*

Shedra – spiritual school

Stupa – funerary mount or monument serving as Buddhist shrine

Sutras – refers to sacred texts of Buddhism

Tantra – teachings related to particular techniques and rituals, especially dealing with meditative practices

Terton – treasure finder

Tsampa – roasted barley flour, the staple food of Tibet

Tulku – recognized reincarnated being

Yetis – primitive snowpeople

Zhen – loose-fitting upper garment

BIBLIOGRAPHY

Ajit Mookerjee and Madhu Khanna., *The Tantric Way.* Vikas, Delhi, 1977.

Avedon, John F., *In Exile from the Land of Snows.* Alfred A. Knopf, New York, 1984.

Dalai Lama, the Fourteenth, *My Land and My People.* McGraw Hill, New York, 1962.

Dalai Lama, the Fourteenth, *The Buddhism of Tibet and the Key to the Middle Way.* Harper and Row, New York, 1975.

Dhargyey, Geshey Ngawang, *Tibetan Tradition of Mental Development.* Library of Tibetan Works and Archives, Dharamsala, 1974.

Govinda, Lama Anagarika, *Foundations of Tibetan Mysticism.* Rider, London, 1960.

Jig-me Ling-pa, Tulku Thondup, and Brian C. Beresford, *The Dzong-chen Preliminary Practice of the Innermost Essence.* Library of Tibetan Works and Archives, Dharamsala, 1982.

Kensur Lekden, and Jeffrey Hopkins, *Meditations of a Tibetan Tantric Abbot.* Library of Tibetan Works and Archives, Dharamsala, 1974.

Khetsun Sangpo Rinbochay, and Jeffrey Hopkins, *Tantric Practice in Nying-ma.* Rider, London, 1982.

Lati Rinbochay, and Jeffrey Hopkins, *Death, Intermediate State and Rebirth in Tibetan Buddhism.* Rider, London, 1979.

Lessing, F.D. and A.Wayman, *Introduction to the Buddhist Tantric Systems.* Motilal Banarsidass, The Hague, 1968.

Long-ch'en Rb-jam-pa, His Holiness Dudjom Rinpoche, Beru Khyentze Rinpoche, and Alexander Berzin, *An Introduction to Dzog-ch'en, The Four-Themed Precious Garland.* The Library of Tibetan Works and Archives, Dharamsala, 1979.

National Geographic, Vol. LXVIII, No. 4; Vol. XC, No. 2; Vol. CVIII, No. 1; Vol.157, No. 2.

Pal, Pratapaditya, *Tibetan Paintings,* Sotheby Publications, London, 1984.

The Cultural Relics Administration Committee, Tibet Autonomous Region, *The Potala Palace of Tibet.* Joint Publishing Co., Hong Kong, 1982.

Thurman, Robert A.F., *Tibet the Mystic Nation.* Parabola, "Exile" Issue, 1985.

Tsong-ka-pa, and Jeffrey Hopkins, *Tantra in Tibet.* George Allen and Unwin, Ltd., London, 1977.

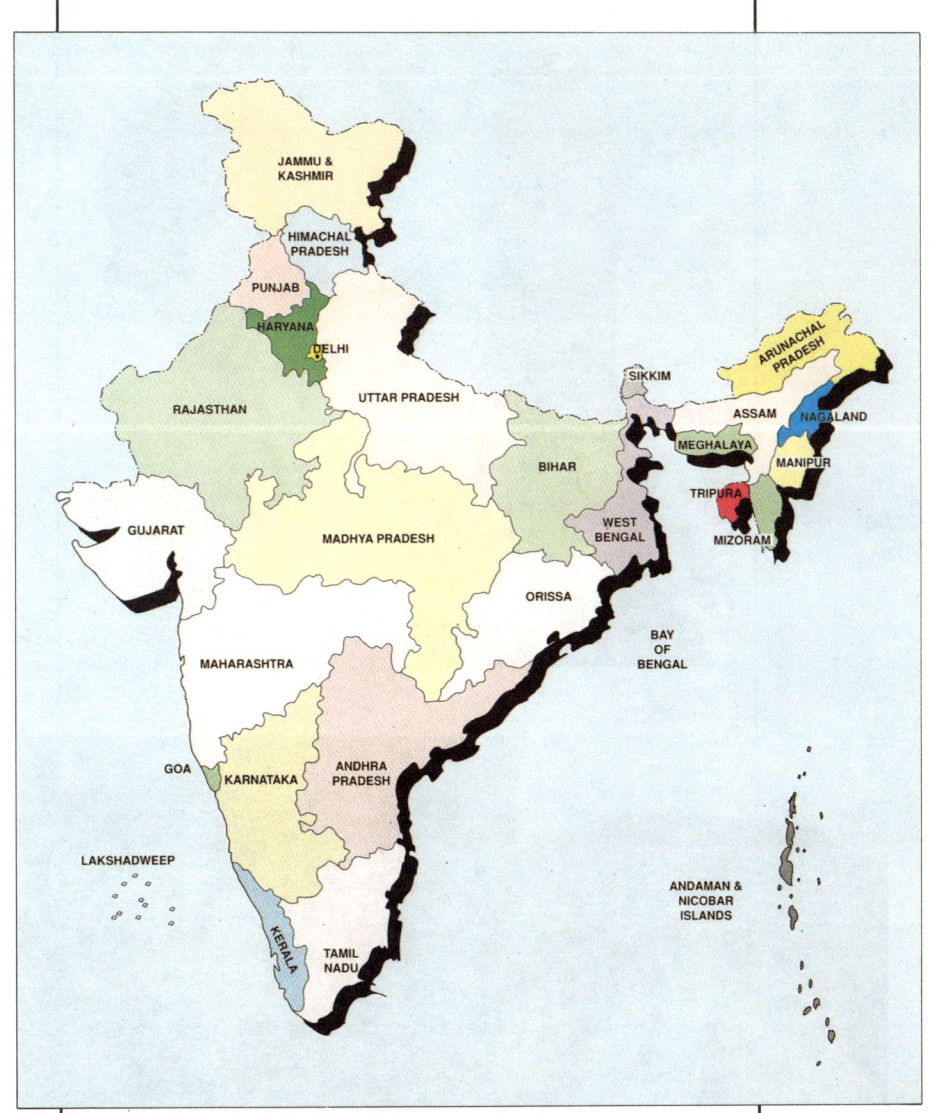

India is a union of twenty–five states and seven centrally–administered union territories. It is the seventh largest nation in the world and is a Sovereign Democratic Republic with a Parliamentary system of government.

Map courtesy of Indian Consulate, New York, 1993

Yeshe Dorje Rinpoche with Dr. Marsha Woolf
Photo by
Bill Coutts

Yeshe Dorje Rinpoche with Professor Karen Blanc
Photo by
David Johnston

ABOUT THE AUTHORS

MARSHA WOOLF is Founder and Director of the New World Medical Center and Alternative Resources in Massachusetts and New York. A Naturopath of twenty-five years and a specialist in Oriental Medicine, she is also the Director of the Tibetan Refugee Alternative Health Care Project.

She has studied with many well-known teachers such as Dr. So Tin Yau, Hong Kong; Michio Kushi, Boston; Dr. Tatsuzo Nakamura, Japan; Dr. Ted Kaptchuk, Cambridge; and Dr. Paul Nogier, France. Her most recent teacher for the past thirteen years is Dr. Yeshi Dhonden, India, former personal physician to His Holiness the Dalai Lama. Her interest in all areas of indigenous and alternative healing practices has led her to study and practice in Europe, Central and South America, India, and the Far East.

KAREN BLANC received her B.A. with honors from Indiana University and her M.A. in English from Columbia University. After graduation, she entered a convent and left during her novitiate to work with the poor in the slums of New York City.

The author of three books, *I, Poem Maker; Dear Hilda;* and *Adventure with a Holy Man,* Professor Blanc is a faculty member at Touro College, School of General Studies, in East Harlem. She has lived and studied with Hilda Charlton in New York, attended courses taught by Sri Sathya Sai Baba in India, and currently teaches prayer and meditation in New York.

The first group of monks to complete the three–year, three–month, three–day retreat at Zilnon Kagyeling Monastery, in the summer of 1990, shown with Yeshe Dorje Rinpoche and Dr. Marsha Woolf
Photo by Karma Sonam

To the left, Yeshe Dorje Rinpoche with his son Venerable Tenzin Sangpo and Dr. Yeshi Dhonden.

Below, Yeshe Dorje Rinpoche with his son Karma Sonam.

Photos by
Dr. Marsha Woolf

Yeshe Dorje Rinpoche with his daughter, Mingur Chodon
Photo by Dr. Marsha Woolf

Yeshe Dorje Rinpoche with his son Karma Norbu
Photo by Dr. Marsha Woolf